INDIAN POETRY

T0352719

Trübner's Oriental Series

INDIA: LANGUAGE AND LITERATURE
In 14 Volumes

INDIAN POETRY

EDWIN ARNOLD

Routledge
Taylor & Francis Group

LONDON AND NEW YORK

First published in 1886 by
Trübner & Co Ltd

Reprinted in 2000 by
Routledge
2 Park Square, Milton Park, Abingdon, Oxon, OX14 4RN

Simultaneously published in the USA and Canada by Routledge

711 Third Avenue, New York, NY 10017

Transferred to Digital Printing 2007

Routledge is an imprint of the Taylor & Francis Group

First issued in paperback 2013

The publishers have made every effort to contact authors/copyright holders
of the works reprinted in *Trübner's Oriental Series*.
This has not been possible in every case, however, and we would
welcome correspondence from those individuals/companies
we have been unable to trace.

These reprints are taken from original copies of each book. In many cases
the condition of these originals is not perfect. The publisher has gone to
great lengths to ensure the quality of these reprints, but wishes to point
out that certain characteristics of the original copies will, of necessity, be
apparent in reprints thereof.

British Library Cataloguing in Publication Data
A CIP catalogue record for this book
is available from the British Library

Indian Poetry
ISBN 978-0-415-24500-5 (hbk)
ISBN 978-0-415-86573-9 (pbk)

INDIAN POETRY

CONTAINING

"THE INDIAN SONG OF SONGS," FROM THE SANSKRIT
OF THE GÎTA GOVINDA OF JAYADEVA
TWO BOOKS FROM "THE ILIAD OF INDIA" (MAHÁBHÁRATA)
"PROVERBIAL WISDOM" FROM THE SHLOKAS OF THE
HITOPADEŚA, AND OTHER ORIENTAL POEMS

BY

SIR EDWIN ARNOLD, M.A., K.C.I.E., C.S.I.

Author of " The Light of Asia"

OFFICER OF THE WHITE ELEPHANT OF SIAM
THIRD CLASS OF THE IMPERIAL ORDER OF THE MEDJIDIE
FELLOW OF THE ROYAL ASIATIC AND ROYAL GEOGRAPHICAL SOCIETIES
HONORARY MEMBER OF THE SOCIÉTÉ DE GEOGRAPHIE, MARSEILLES, ETC. ETC.
FORMERLY PRINCIPAL OF THE DECCAN COLLEGE, POONA
AND FELLOW OF THE UNIVERSITY OF BOMBAY

Fourth Edition

LONDON
TRÜBNER & CO., LUDGATE HILL

CONTENTS.

CONTENTS.

THE INDIAN SONG OF SONGS.

——o——

OM!

REVERENCE TO GANESHA!

" THE sky is clouded; and the wood resembles
    The sky, thick-arched with black Tamâla boughs;
O Radha, Radha! take this Soul, that trembles
    In life's deep midnight, to Thy golden house."
So Nanda spoke,—and, led by Radha's spirit,
    The feet of Krishna found the road aright;
Wherefore, in bliss which all high hearts inherit,
    Together taste they Love's divine delight.

He who wrote these things for thee,
Of the Son of Wassoodee,

A

Was the poet Jayadeva ;
Him Saraswati gave ever
Fancies fair his mind to throng,
Like pictures palace-walls along ;
Ever to his notes of love
Lakshmi's mystic dancers move.
If thy spirit seeks to brood
On Hari glorious, Hari good ;
If it feeds on solemn numbers,
Dim as dreams and soft as slumbers,
Lend thine ear to Jayadev,
Lord of all the spells that save.
Umapatidhara's strain
Glows like roses after rain ;
Sharan's stream-like song is grand,
If its tide ye understand ;
Bard more wise beneath the sun
Is not found than Govardhun :
Dhoyi holds the listener still
With his shlokes of subtle skill ;
But for sweet words suited well
Jayadeva doth excel.

(*What follows is to the Music* MÂLAVA *and the Mode*
RUPAKA.)

HYMN TO VISHNU.

O thou that held'st the blessèd Veda dry
    When all things else beneath the floods were hurled;
Strong Fish-God! Ark of Men! *Jai!* Hari, *jai!*
    Hail, Keshav, hail! thou Master of the world!

The round world rested on thy spacious nape;
    Upon thy neck, like a mere mole, it stood:
O thou that took'st for us the Tortoise-shape,
    Hail, Keshav, hail! Ruler of wave and wood!

The world upon thy curving tusk sate sure,
    Like the Moon's dark disc in her crescent pale;
O thou who didst for us assume the Boar,
    Immortal Conqueror! hail, Keshav, hail!

When thou thy Giant-Foe didst seize and rend,
    Fierce, fearful, long, and sharp were fang and nail;
Thou who the Lion and the Man didst blend,
    Lord of the Universe! hail, Narsingh, hail!

Wonderful Dwarf !—who with a threefold stride
  Cheated King Bali—where thy footsteps fall
Men's sins, O Wamuna ! are set aside :
  O Keshav, hail ! thou Help and Hope of all !

The sins of this sad earth thou didst assoil,
  The anguish of its creatures thou didst heal ;
Freed are we from all terrors by thy toil :
  Hail, Purshuram, hail ! Lord of the biting steel !

To thee the fell Ten-Headed yielded life,
  Thou in dread battle laid'st the monster low !
Ah, Rama ! dear to Gods and men that strife ;
  We praise thee, Master of the matchless bow !

With clouds for garments glorious thou dost fare,
  Veiling thy dazzling majesty and might,
As when Yamuna saw thee with the share,
  A peasant—yet the King of Day and Night.

Merciful-hearted ! when thou camest as Boodh—
  Albeit 'twas written in the Scriptures so—
Thou bad'st our altars be no more imbrued
  With blood of victims : Keshav ! bending low—

We praise thee, Wielder of the sweeping sword,
   Brilliant as curving comets in the gloom,
Whose edge shall smite the fierce barbarian horde;
   Hail to thee, Keshav! hail, and hear, and come,

And fill this song of Jayadev with thee,
   And make it wise to teach, strong to redeem,
And sweet to living souls. Thou Mystery!
   Thou Light of Life! Thou Dawn beyond the dream!

     Fish! that didst outswim the flood;
     Tortoise! whereon earth hath stood;
     Boar! who with thy tush held'st high
     The world, that mortals might not die;
     Lion! who hast giants torn;
     Dwarf! who laugh'dst a king to scorn;
     Sole Subduer of the Dreaded!
     Slayer of the many-headed!
     Mighty Ploughman! Teacher tender!
     Of thine own the sure Defender!
     Under all thy ten disguises
     Endless praise to thee arises.

(What follows is to the Music GURJJARÎ *and the Mode* NIHSÂRA.)

Endless praise arises,
O thou God that liest
Rapt, on Kumla's breast,
Happiest, holiest, highest!
Planets are thy jewels,
Stars thy forehead-gems,
Set like sapphires gleaming
In kingliest anadems;
Even the great gold Sun-God,
Blazing through the sky,
Serves thee but for crest-stone,
Jai, jai! Hari, *jai!*
As that Lord of day
After night brings morrow,
Thou dost charm away
Life's long dream of sorrow.
As on Mansa's water
Brood the swans at rest,
So thy laws sit stately
On a holy breast.

O, Drinker of the poison!

Ah, high Delight of earth!

What light is to the lotus-buds,

What singing is to mirth,

Art thou—art thou that slayedst

Madhou and Narak grim;

That ridest on the King of Birds,

Making all glories dim.

With eyes like open lotus-flowers,

Bright in the morning rain,

Freeing by one swift piteous glance

The spirit from Life's pain:

Of all the three Worlds Treasure!

Of sin the Putter-by!

O'er the Ten-Headed Victor!

Jai Hari! Hari! *jai!*

Thou Shaker of the Mountain!

Thou Shadow of the Storm!

Thou Cloud that unto Lakshmi's face

Comes welcome, white, and warm!

O thou,—who to great Lakshmi

Art like the silvery beam

Which moon-sick chakors feed upor

By Jumna's silent stream,—
To thee this hymn ascendeth,
That Jayadev doth sing,
Of worship, love, and mystery;
High Lord and heavenly King!
And unto whoso hears it
Do thou a blessing bring—
Whose neck is gilt with yellow dust
From lilies that did cling
Beneath the breasts of Lakshmi,
A girdle soft and sweet,
When in divine embracing
The lips of Gods did meet;
And the beating heart above
Of thee—Dread Lord of Heaven!—
She left that stamp of love—
By such deep sign be given
Prays Jayadev, the glory
And the secret and the spells
Which close-hid in this story
Unto wise ears he tells.

END OF INTRODUCTION.

SARGA THE FIRST.

—o—

S A M O D A D A M O D A R O.

THE SPORTS OF KRISHNA.

BEAUTIFUL Radha, jasmine-bosomed Radha,
All in the Spring-time waited by the wood
For Krishna fair, Krishna the all-forgetful,—
Krishna with earthly love's false fire consuming—
And some one of her maidens sang this song:—

(*What follows is to the Music* VASANTA *and the Mode*
YATI.)

I know where Krishna tarries in these early days of
    Spring,
When every wind from warm Malay brings fragrance
    on its wing;

Brings fragrance stolen far away from thickets of the
    clove,
In jungles where the bees hum and the Koïl flutes her
    love;
He dances with the dancers, of a merry morrice one,
All in the budding Spring-time, for 'tis sad to be alone.

I know how Krishna passes these hours of blue and gold,
When parted lovers sigh to meet and greet and closely
    hold
Hand fast in hand; and every branch upon the Vakul-
    tree
Droops downward with a hundred blooms, in every
    bloom a bee;
He is dancing with the dancers to a laughter-moving
    tone,
In the soft awakening Spring-time, when 'tis hard to
    live alone.

Where Kroona-flowers, that open at a lover's lightest
    tread,
Break, and, for shame at what they hear, from white
    blush modest red;

And all the spears on all the boughs of all the Ketuk-
    glades
Seem ready darts to pierce the hearts of wandering
    youths and maids;
'Tis there thy Krishna dances till the merry drum is
    done,
All in the sunny Spring-time, when who can live alone?

Where the breaking forth of blossom on the yellow
    Keshra-sprays
Dazzles like Kama's sceptre, whom all the world obeys;
And Pâtal-buds fill drowsy bees from pink delicious
    bowls,
As Kama's nectared goblet steeps in languor human
    souls;
There he dances with the dancers, and of Radha thinketh
    none,
All in the warm new Spring-tide, when none will live
    alone.

Where the breath of waving Mâdhvi pours incense
    through the grove,
And silken Mogras lull the sense with essences of
    love,—

The silken-soft pale Mogra, whose perfume fine and faint

Can melt the coldness of a maid, the sternness of a
saint—

There dances with those dancers thine other self, thine
Own,

All in the languorous Spring-time, when none will live
alone.

Where—as if warm lips touched sealed eyes and waked
them—all the bloom

Opens upon the mangoes to feel the sunshine come;

And Atimuktas wind their arms of softest green about,

Clasping the stems, while calm and clear great Jumna
spreadeth out;

There dances and there laughs thy Love, with damsels
many an one,

In the rosy days of Spring-time, for he will not live
alone.

Mark this song of Jayadev !
Deep as pearl in ocean-wave
Lurketh in its lines a wonder
Which the wise alone will ponder:

Though it seemeth of the earth,
Heavenly is the music's birth ;
Telling darkly of delights
In the wood, of wasted nights,
Of witless days, and fruitless love,
And false pleasures of the grove,
And rash passions of the prime,
And those dances of Spring-time ;
Time, which seems so subtle-sweet,
Time, which pipes to dancing-feet,
Ah ! so softly—ah ! so sweetly—
That among those wood-maids featly
Krishna cannot choose but dance,
Letting pass life's greater chance.

Yet the winds that sigh so
   As they stir the rose,
Wake a sigh from Krishna
   Wistfuller than those;
All their faint breaths swinging
   The creepers to and fro
Pass like rustling arrows
   Shot from Kama's bow:

Thus among the dancers
    What those zephyrs bring
Strikes to Krishna's spirit
    Like a darted sting.

And all as if—far wandered—
    The traveller should hear
The bird of home, the Koïl,
    With nest-notes rich and clear;
And there should come one moment
    A blessèd fleeting dream
Of the bees among the mangoes
    Beside his native stream;
So flash those sudden yearnings,
    That sense of a dearer thing,
The love and lack of Radha
    Upon his soul in Spring.

Then she, the maid of Radha, spake again;
And pointing far away between the leaves
Guided her lovely Mistress where to look,
And note how Krishna wantoned in the wood
Now with this one, now that; his heart, her prize,

Panting with foolish passions, and his eyes

Beaming with too much love for those fair girls—

Fair, but not so as Radha; and she sang:

(*What follows is to the Music* Râmagirî *and the Mode*
Yati.)

See, Lady! how thy Krishna passes these idle hours

Decked forth in fold of woven gold, and crowned with
forest-flowers;

And scented with the sandal, and gay with gems of
price—

Rubies to mate his laughing lips, and diamonds like his
eyes;—

In the company of damsels,* who dance and sing and
play,

Lies Krishna, laughing, toying, dreaming his Spring away.

One, with star-blossomed champâk wreathed, wooes
him to rest his head

On the dark pillow of her breast so tenderly outspread;

---

* It will be observed that the "Gopis" here personify the five
senses. Lassen says, "*Manifestum est puellis istis nil aliud significari
quam res sensiles.*"

And o'er his brow with roses blown she fans a fragrance
    rare,

That falls on the enchanted sense like rain in thirsty air,

While the company of damsels wave many an odorous
    spray,

And Krishna, laughing, toying, sighs the soft Spring
    away.

Another, gazing in his face, sits wistfully apart,

Searching it with those looks of love that leap from
    heart to heart;

Her eyes—afire with shy desire, veiled by their lashes
    black—

Speak so that Krishna cannot choose but send the
    message back,

In the company of damsels whose bright eyes in a ring

Shine round him with soft meanings in the merry light
    of Spring.

The third one of that dazzling band of dwellers in the
    wood—

Body and bosom panting with the pulse of youthful
    blood—

Leans over him, as in his ear a lightsome thing to
    speak,
And then with leaf-soft lip imprints a kiss below his
    cheek ;
A kiss that thrills, and Krishna turns at the silken touch
To give it back—ah, Radha! forgetting thee too much.

And one with arch smile becokns him away from
    Jumna's banks,
Where the tall bamboos bristle like spears in battle-
    ranks,
And plucks his cloth to make him come into the mango-
    shade,
Where the fruit is ripe and golden, and the milk and
    cakes are laid :
Oh! golden-red the mangoes, and glad the feasts of
    Spring,
And fair the flowers to lie upon, and sweet the dancers
    sing.

Sweetest of all that Temptress who dances for him now
With subtle feet which part and meet in the Râs-
    measure slow,

B

To the chime of silver bangles and the beat of rose-leaf
    hands,

And pipe and lute and cymbal played by the woodland
    bands;

So that wholly passion-laden—eye, ear, sense, soul o'er-
    come—

Krishna is theirs in the forest; his heart forgets its home.

Krishna, made for heavenly things,
'Mid those woodland singers sings;
With those dancers dances featly,
Gives back soft embraces sweetly;
Smiles on that one, toys with this,
Glance for glance and kiss for kiss;
Meets the merry damsels fairly,
Plays the round of folly rarely,
Lapped in milk-warm spring-time weather,
He and those brown girls together.

And this shadowed earthly love
In the twilight of the grove,
Dance and song and soft caresses,
Meeting looks and tangled tresses,

Jayadev the same hath writ,
That ye might have gain of it,
Sagely its deep sense conceiving
And its inner light believing;
How that Love—the mighty Master,
Lord of all the stars that cluster
In the sky, swiftest and slowest,
Lord of highest, Lord of lowest—
Manifests himself to mortals,
Winning them towards the portals
Of his secret House, the gates
Of that bright Paradise which waits
The wise in love. Ah, human creatures!
Even your phantasies are teachers.
Mighty Love makes sweet in seeming
Even Krishna's woodland dreaming;
Mighty Love sways all alike
From self to selflessness. Oh! strike
From your eyes the veil, and see
What Love willeth Him to be
Who in error, but in grace,
Sitteth with that lotus-face,
And those eyes whose rays of heaven
Unto phantom-eyes are given;

Holding feasts of foolish mirth
With these Visions of the earth ;
Learning love, and love imparting ;
Yet with sense of loss upstarting :—

For the cloud that veils the fountains
Underneath the Sandal mountains,
How—as if the sunshine drew
All its being to the blue—
It takes flight, and seeks to rise
High into the purer skies,
High into the snow and frost,
On the shining summits lost !
Ah ! and how the Koïl's strain
Smites the traveller with pain,—
When the mango blooms in spring,
And " Koohoo," " Koohoo," they sing—
Pain of pleasures not yet won,
Pain of journeys not yet done,
Pain of toiling without gaining,
Pain, 'mid gladness, of still paining.

But may He guide us all to glory high
Who laughed when Radha glided, hidden, by,
And all among those damsels free and bold
Touched Krishna with a soft mouth, kind and cold ;
And like the others, leaning on his breast,
Unlike the others, left there Love's unrest ;
And like the others, joining in his song,
Unlike the others, made him silent long.

(Here ends that Sarga of the Gîta Govinda entitled
SAMODADAMODARO.)

SARGA THE SECOND.

——◦——

KLESHAKESHAVO.

THE PENITENCE OF KRISHNA.

THUS lingered Krishna in the deep, green wood,
And gave himself, too prodigal, to those;
But Radha, heart-sick at his falling-off,
Seeing her heavenly beauty slighted so,
Withdrew; and, in a bower of Paradise—
Where nectarous blossoms wove a shrine of shade,
Haunted by birds and bees of unknown skies—
She sate deep-sorrowful, and sang this strain:

(*What follows is to the Music* GURJJARÎ *and the Mode*
YATI.)

Ah, my Beloved! taken with those glances,
Ah, my Beloved! dancing those rash dances,

Ah, Minstrel! playing wrongful strains so well;
Ah, Krishna! Krishna, with the honeyed lip!
Ah, Wanderer into foolish fellowship!
   My Dancer, my Delight!—I love thee still.

O Dancer! strip thy peacock-crown away,
Rise! thou whose forehead is the star of day,
   With beauty for its silver halo set;
Come! thou whose greatness gleams beneath its shroud
Like Indra's rainbow shining through the cloud—
   Come, for I love thee, my Beloved! yet.

Must love thee—cannot choose but love thee ever,
My best Beloved!—set on this endeavour,
   To win thy tender heart and earnest eye
From lips but sadly sweet, from restless bosoms,
To mine, O Krishna with the mouth of blossoms!
   To mine, thou soul of Krishna! yet I sigh

Half hopeless, thinking of myself forsaken,
And thee, dear Loiterer, in the wood o'ertaken
   With passion for those bold and wanton ones,

Who knit thine arms as poison-plants gripe trees
With twining cords—their flowers the braveries
   That flash in the green gloom, sparkling stars and
      stones.

My Prince! my Lotus-faced! my woe! my love!
Whose broad brow, with the tilka-spot above,
   Shames the bright moon at full with fleck of cloud;
Thou to mistake so little for so much!
Thou, Krishna, to be palm to palm with such!
   O Soul made for my joys, pure, perfect, proud!

Ah, my Beloved! in thy darkness dear;
Ah, Dancer! with the jewels in thine ear,
   Swinging to music of a loveless love;
O my Beloved! in thy fall so high
That angels, sages, spirits of the sky
   Linger about thee, watching in the grove.

I will be patient still, and draw thee ever,
My one Beloved, sitting by the river
   Under the thick kadambas with that throng:

Will there not come an end to earthly madness?

Shall I not, past the sorrow, have the gladness?

  Must not the love-light shine for him ere long?

> *Shine, thou Light by Radha given,*
>
> *Shine, thou splendid star of heaven!*
>
> *Be a lamp to Krishna's feet,*
>
> *Show to all hearts secrets sweet,*
>
> *Of the wonder and the love*
>
> *Jayadev hath writ above.*
>
> *Be the quick Interpreter*
>
> *Unto wisest ears of her*
>
> *Who always sings to all, " I wait,*
>
> *He loveth still who loveth late."*

For (sang on that high Lady in the shade)

My soul for tenderness, not blame, was made;

  Mine eyes look through his evil to his good;

My heart coins pleas for him; my fervent thought

Prevents what he will say when these are naught,

  And that which I am shall be understood.

Then spake she to her maiden wistfully—

(What follows is to the Music Mâlavagauda *and the*
Mode Ekatâlî.*)*

Go to him,—win him hither,—whisper low
   How he may find me if he searches well;
Say, if he will—joys past his hope to know
   Await him here; go now to him, and tell
Where Radha is, and that henceforth she charms
       His spirit to her arms.

Yes, go! say, if he will, that he may come—
   May come, my love, my longing, my desire;
May come forgiven, shriven, to me his home,
   And make his happy peace; nay, and aspire
To uplift Radha's veil, and learn at length
       What love is in its strength.

Lead him; say softly I shall chide his blindness,
   And vex him with my angers; yet add this,
He shall not vainly sue for loving-kindness,
   Nor miss to see me close, nor lose the bliss
That lives upon my lip, nor be denied
       The rose-throne at my side.

Say that I—Radha—in my bower languish
   All widowed, till he find the way to me;
Say that mine eyes are dim, my breast all anguish,
   Until with gentle murmured shame I see
His steps come near, his anxious pleading face
             Bend for my pardoning grace.

While I—what, did he deem light loves so tender,
   To tarry for them when the vow was made
To yield him up my bosom's maiden splendour,
   And fold him in my fragrance, and unbraid
My shining hair for him, and clasp him close
            To the gold heart of his Rose ?

And sing him strains which only spirits know,
   And make him captive with the silk-soft chain
Of twinned-wings brooding round him, and bestow
   Kisses of Paradise, as pure as rain ;
My gems, my moonlight-pearls, my girdle-gold,
            Cymbaling music bold ?

While gained for ever, I shall dare to grow
   Life to life with him, in the realms divine ;

And—Love's large cup at happy overflow,
   Yet ever to be filled—his eyes and mine
Will meet in that glad look, when Time's great gate
      Closes and shuts out Fate.

      Listen to the unsaid things
      Of the song that Radha sings,
      For the soul draws near to bliss,
      As it comprehendeth this.
      I am Jayadev, who write
      All this subtle-rich delight
      For your teaching.   Ponder, then,
      What it tells to Gods and men.
      Err not, watching Krishna gay,
      With those brown girls all at play;
      Understand how Radha charms
      Her wandering lover to her arms,
      Waiting with divinest love
      Till his dream ends in the grove.

For even now (she sang) I see him pause,
   Heart-stricken with the waste of heart he makes

Amid them;—all the bows of their bent brows

Wound him no more: no more for all their sakes

Plays he one note upon his amorous lute,

But lets the strings lie mute.

Pensive, as if his parted lips should say—

" My feet with the dances are weary,

The music has dropped from the song,

There is no more delight in the lute-strings,

Sweet Shadows! what thing has gone wrong?

The wings of the wind have left fanning

The palms of the glade;

They are dead, and the blossoms seem dying

In the place where we played.

" We will play no more, beautiful Shadows!

A fancy came solemn and sad,

More sweet, with unspeakable longings,

Than the best of the pleasures we had:

I am not now the Krishna who kissed you;

That exquisite dream,—

The Vision I saw in my dancing—

Has spoiled what you seem.

"Ah! delicate phantoms that cheated
    With eyes that looked lasting and true,
I awake,—I have seen her,—my angel—
    Farewell to the wood and to you!
Oh, whisper of wonderful pity!
    Oh, fair face that shone!
Though thou be a vision, Divinest!
    This vision is done."

(*Here ends that Sarga of the Gîta Govinda entitled*
KLESHAKESHAVO.)

SARGA THE THIRD.

———o———

MUGDHAMADHUSUDANO.

KRISHNA TROUBLED.

THEREAT,—as one who welcomes to her throne
A new-made Queen, and brings before it bound
Her enemies,—so Krishna in his heart
Throned Radha; and—all treasonous follies chained—
He played no more with those first play-fellows:
But, searching through the shadows of the grove
For loveliest Radha,—when he found her not,
Faint with the quest, despairing, lonely, lorn,
And pierced with shame for wasted love and days,
He sate by Jumna, where the canes are thick,
And sang to the wood-echoes words like these:

(*What follows is to the Music* GURJJARÎ *and to the Mode*
YATI.)

Radha, Enchantress! Radha, queen of all!
   Gone—lost, because she found me sinning here;
And I so stricken with my foolish fall,
    I could not stay her out of shame and fear;
                She will not hear;
    In her disdain and grief vainly I call.

And if she heard, what would she do? what say?
   How could I make it good that I forgot?
What profit was it to me, night and day,
    To live, love, dance, and dream, having her not?
            Soul without spot!
I wronged thy patience, till it sighed away.

Sadly I know the truth. Ah! even now
   Remembering that one look beside the river,
Softer the vexed eyes seem, and the proud brow
    Than lotus-leaves when the bees make them quiver.
             My love for ever!
Too late is Krishna wise—too far art thou!

Yet all day long in my deep heart I woo thee,

    And all night long with thee my dreams are sweet;

Why, then, so vainly must my steps pursue thee?

    Why can I never reach thee, to entreat,

              Low at thy feet,

Dear vanished Splendour! till my tears subdue thee?

Surpassing One! I knew thou didst not brook

    Half-hearted worship, and a love that wavers;

Haho! there is the wisdom I mistook,

    Therefore I seek with desperate endeavours;

              That fault dissevers

Me from my heaven, astray—condemned—forsook!

And yet I seem to feel, to know, thee near me;

    Thy steps make music, measured music, near;

Radha! my Radha! will not sorrow clear me?

    Shine once! speak one word pitiful and dear!

              Wilt thou not hear?

Canst thou—because I did forget—forsake me?

Forgive! the sin is sinned, is past, is over;

    No thought I think shall do thee wrong again;

                          c

Turn thy dark eyes again upon thy lover
    Bright Spirit! or I perish of this pain.
                Loving again!
In dread of doom to love, but not recover.

So did Krishna sing and sigh
By the river-bank; and I,
Jayadev of Kinduvilva,
Resting—as the moon of silver
Sits upon the solemn ocean—
On full faith, in deep devotion;
Tell it that ye may perceive
How the heart must fret and grieve;
How the soul doth tire of earth,
When the love from Heav'n hath birth.

For (sang he on) I am no foe of thine,
    There is no black snake, Kama! in my hair;
Blue lotus-bloom, and not the poisoned brine,
        Shadows my neck; what stains my bosom bare,
                Thou God unfair!
Is sandal-dust, not ashes; nought of mine

Makes me like Shiva that thou, Lord of Love!
  Shouldst strain thy string at me and fit thy dart;
This world is thine—let be one breast thereof
  Which bleeds already, wounded to the heart
        With lasting smart,
Shot from those brows that did my sin reprove.

Thou gavest her those black brows for a bow
  Arched like thine own, whose pointed arrows seem
Her glances, and the underlids that go—
  So firm and fine—its string? Ah, fleeting gleam!
        Beautiful dream!
Small need of Kama's help hast thou, I trow,

To smite me to the soul with love;—but set
  Those arrows to their silken cord! enchain
My thoughts in that loose hair! let thy lips, wet
  With dew of heaven as bimba-buds with rain,
        Bloom precious pain
Of longing in my heart; and, keener yet,

The heaving of thy lovely, angry bosom,
  Pant to my spirit things unseen, unsaid;

But if thy touch, thy tones, if the dark blossom
Of thy dear face, thy jasmine-odours shed
From feet to head,
If these be all with me, canst thou be far—be fled ?

So sang he, and I pray that whoso hears
The music of his burning hopes and fears,
That whoso sees this vision by the River
Of Krishna, Hari, (can we name him ever ?)
And marks his ear-ring rubies swinging slow,
As he sits still, unheedful, bending low
To play this tune upon his lute, while all
Listen to catch the sadness musical ;
And Krishna wotteth nought, but, with set face
Turned full toward Radha's, sings on in that place ;
May all such souls—prays Jayadev—be wise
To learn the wisdom which hereunder lies.

(*Here ends that Sarga of the Gîta Govinda entitled*
MUGDHAMADHUSUDANO.)

SARGA THE FOURTH.

—o—

SNIGDHAMADHUSUDANO.

KRISHNA CHEERED.

THEN she whom Radha sent came to the canes—
The canes beside the river where he lay
With listless limbs and spirit weak from love;—
And she sang this to Krishna wistfully:

(What follows is to the Music KARNÂTA *and the Mode*
EKATÂLÎ.*)*

Art thou sick for Radha? she is sad in turn,
  Heaven foregoes its blessings, if it holds not thee;
All the cooling fragrance of sandal she doth spurn,
  Moonlight makes her mournful with radiance silvery;

Even the southern breeze blown fresh from pearly seas,
  Seems to her but tainted by a dolorous brine;
And for thy sake discontented, with a great love over-
    laden,
    Her soul comes here beside thee, and sitteth down
      with thine.

Her soul comes here beside thee, and tenderly and true
  It weaves a subtle mail of proof to ward off sin and
    pain;
A breastplate soft as lotus-leaf, with holy tears for dew,
  To guard thee from the things that hurt; and then
    'tis gone again
To strew a blissful place with the richest buds that grace
  Kama's sweet world, a meeting-spot with rose and
    jasmine fair,
For the hour when, well-contented, with a love no
    longer troubled,
  Thou shalt find the way to Radha, and finish sorrows
    there.

But now her lovely face is shadowed by her fears;
  Her glorious eyes are veiled and dim like moonlight
    in eclipse

By breaking rain-clouds, Krishna! yet she paints you
     in her tears
  With tender thoughts—not Krishna, but brow and
     breast and lips
And form and mien a King, a great and god-like thing;
  And then with bended head she asks grace from the
     Love Divine,
To keep thee discontented with the phantoms thou for-
     swearest,
  Till she may win her glory, and thou be raised to thine.

       Softly now she sayeth,
         " Krishna, Krishna, come!"
       Lovingly she prayeth,
         " Fair moon, light him home."
       Yet if Hari helps not,
         Moonlight cannot aid;
       Ah! the woeful Radha!
         Ah! the forest shade!

       Ah! if Hari guide not,
         Moonlight is as gloom;
       Ah! if moonlight help not,
         How shall Krishna come?

Sad for Krishna grieving
In the darkened grove;
Sad for Radha weaving
Dreams of fruitless love!

Strike soft strings to this soft measure,
If thine ear would catch its treasure;
Slowly dance to this deep song,
Let its meaning float along
With grave paces, since it tells
Of a love that sweetly dwells
In a tender distant glory,
Past all faults of mortal story.

(*What follows is to the Music* DESHÂGA *and the Mode*
EKATÂLÎ.)

Krishna, till thou come unto her, faint she lies with
love and fear;

Even the jewels of her necklet seem a load too great to
bear.

Krishna, till thou come unto her, all the sandal and the
flowers

Vex her with their pure perfection though they grow in
heavenly bowers.

Krishna, till thou come unto her, fair albeit those
    bowers may be,
Passion burns her, and love's fire fevers her for lack of
    thee.

Krishna, till thou come unto her, those divine lids, dark
    and tender,
Droop like lotus-leaves in rain-storms, dashed and heavy
    in their splendour.

Krishna, till thou come unto her, that rose-couch which
    she hath spread
Saddens with its empty place, its double pillow for one
    head.
Krishna, till thou come unto her, from her palms she
    will not lift

The dark face hidden deep within them like the moon
    in cloudy rift.

Krishna, till thou come unto her, angel though she be,
    thy Love
Sighs and suffers, waits and watches—joyless 'mid those
    joys above.

Krishna, till thou come unto her, with the comfort of
thy kiss

Deeper than thy loss, O Krishna! must be loss of
Radha's bliss.

Krishna, while thou didst forget her—her, thy life, thy
gentle fate—

Wonderful her waiting was, her pity sweet, her patience
great.

Krishna, come! 'tis grief untold to grieve her—shame
to let her sigh;

Come, for she is sick with love, and thou her only
remedy.

So she sang, and Jayadeva
Prays for all, and prays for ever,
That Great Hari may bestow
Utmost bliss of loving so
On us all;—that one who wore
The herdsman's form, and heretofore,
To save the shepherd's threatened flock,
Up from the earth reared the huge rock—

Bestow it with a gracious hand,

Albeit, amid the woodland band,

Clinging close in fond caresses

Krishna gave them ardent kisses,

Taking on his lips divine

Earthly stamp and woodland sign.

(Here ends that Sarga of the Gîta Govinda entitled Snigdhamadhusudano).

SARGA THE FIFTH.

——o——

SAKANDKṢHAPUNDARIKAKSHO.

THE LONGINGS OF KRISHNA.

" SAY I am here! oh, if she pardons me,
  Say where I am, and win her softly hither."
So Krishna to the maid; and willingly
She came again to Radha, and she sang:

(*What follows is to the Music* DESHIVARÂDÎ *and the
  Mode* RUPAKA.)

Low whispers the wind from Malaya
    Overladen with love;
On the hills all the grass is burned yellow;
    And the trees in the grove

Droop with tendrils that mock by their clinging
    The thoughts of the parted;
And there lies, sore-sighing for thee,
    Thy love, altered-hearted.

To him the moon's icy-chill silver
    Is a sun at midday;
The fever he burns with is deeper
    Than starlight can stay:
Like one who falls stricken by arrows,
    With the colour departed
From all but his red wounds, so lies
    Thy love, bleeding-hearted.

To the music the banded bees make him
    He closeth his ear;
In the blossoms their small horns are blowing
    The honey-song clear;
But as if every sting to his bosom
    Its smart had imparted,
Low lies by the edge of the river,
    Thy love, aching-hearted.

By the edge of the river, far wandered
  From his once beloved bowers,
And the haunts of his beautiful playmates,
  And the beds strewn with flowers;
Now thy name is his playmate—that only!—
  And the hard rocks upstarted
From the sand make the couch where he lies,
  Thy Krishna, sad-hearted.

Oh may Hari fill each soul,
As these gentle verses roll
Telling of the anguish borne
By kindred ones asunder torn!
Oh may Hari unto each
All the lore of loving teach,
All the pain and all the bliss;
Jayadeva prayeth this!

Yea, Lady! in the self-same spot he waits
Where with thy kiss thou taught'st him utmost love,
And drew him, as none else draws, with thy look;
And all day long, and all night long, his cry
Is "Radha, Radha," like a spell said o'er;

And in his heart there lives no wish nor hope
Save only this, to slake his spirit's thirst
For Radha's love with Radha's lips; and find
Peace on the immortal beauty of thy breast.

(*What follows is to the Music* GURJJARÎ *and the Mode*
EKATÂLÎ.)

Mistress, sweet and bright and holy!
  Meet him in that place;
Change his cheerless melancholy
  Into joy and grace;
If thou hast forgiven, vex not;
  If thou lovest, go,
Watching ever by the river,
  Krishna listens low:

Listens low, and on his reed there
  Softly sounds thy name,
Making even mute things plead there
  For his hope: 'tis shame
That, while winds are welcome to him,
  If from thee they blow,
Mournful ever by the river
  Krishna waits thee so!

When a bird's wing stirs the roses,
   When a leaf falls dead,
Twenty times he recomposes
   The flower-seat he has spread:
Twenty times, with anxious glances
   Seeking thee in vain,
Sighing ever by the river,
   Krishna droops again.

Loosen from thy foot the bangle,
   Lest its golden bell,
With a tiny, tattling jangle,
   Any false tale tell:
If thou fearest that the moonlight
   Will thy glad face know,
Draw those dark braids lower, Lady!
   But to Krishna go.

Swift and still as lightning's splendour
   Let thy beauty come,
Sudden, gracious, dazzling, tender,
   To his arms—its home.

Swift as Indra's yellow lightning,
    Shining through the night,
Glide to Krishna's lonely bosom,
    Take him love and light.

Grant, at last, love's utmost measure,
    Giving, give the whole;
Keep back nothing of the treasure
    Of thy priceless soul:
Hold with both hands out unto him
    Thy chalice, let him drain
The nectar of its dearest draught,
    Till not a wish remain.

Only go—the stars are setting,
    And thy Krishna grieves;
Doubt and anger quite forgetting,
    Hasten through the leaves:
Wherefore didst thou lead him heav'nward
    But for this thing's sake?
Comfort him with pity, Radha!
    Or his heart must break.

D

But while Jayadeva writes
This rare tale of deep delights—
Jayadev, whose heart is given
Unto Hari, Lord in Heaven—
See that ye too, as ye read,
With a glad and humble heed,
Bend your brows before His face,
That ye may have bliss and grace.

And then the Maid, compassionate, sang on—

Lady, most sweet!
For thy coming feet
He listens in the wood, with love sore-tried;
Faintly sighing,
Like one a-dying,
He sends his thoughts afoot to meet his bride.

Ah, silent one!
Sunk is the sun,
The darkness falls as deep as Krishna's sorrow;
The chakor's strain
Is not more vain
Than mine, and soon gray dawn will bring white
morrow.

And thine own bliss

Delays by this;

The utmost of thy heaven comes only so

When, with hearts beating

And passionate greeting,

Parting is over, and the parted grow

One—one for ever!

And the old endeavour

To be so blended is assuaged at last;

And the glad tears raining

Have nought remaining

Of doubt or 'plaining; and the dread has passed

Out of each face,

In the close embrace,

That by-and-by embracing will be over;

The ache that causes

Those mournful pauses

In bowers of earth between lover and lover:

To be no more felt,

To fade, to melt

In the strong certainty of joys immortal;

In the glad meeting,

And quick sweet greeting

Of lips that close beyond Time's shadowy portal.

And to thee is given,

Angel of Heaven!

This glory and this joy with Krishna.   Go!

Let him attain,

For his long pain,

The prize it promised,—see thee coming slow,

A vision first, but then—

By glade and glen—

A lovely, loving soul, true to its home;

His Queen—his Crown—his All,

Hast'ning at last to fall

Upon his breast, and live there.   Radha, come!

Come! and come thou, Lord of all,

Unto whom the Three Worlds call;

Thou, that didst in angry might,

Kansa, like a comet, smite;

Thou, that in thy passion tender,

As incarnate spell and splendour,

Hung on Radha's glorious face—
In the garb of Krishna's grace—
As above the bloom the bee,
When the honeyed revelry
Is too subtle-sweet an one
Not to hang and dally on ;
Thou that art the Three Worlds' glory,
Of life the light, of every story
The meaning and the mark, of love
The root and flower, o' the sky above
The blue, of bliss the heart, of those,
The lovers, that which did impose
The gentle law, that each should be
The other's Heav'n and harmony.

(Here ends that Sarga of the Gîta Govinda entitled
SAKANDKSHAPUNDARIKAKSHO.)

SARGA THE SIXTH.

—— o ——

D H R I S H T A V A I K U N T O.

KRISHNA MADE BOLDER.

But seeing that, for all her loving will,
The flower-soft feet of Radha had not power
To leave their place and go, she sped again—
That maiden—and to Krishna's eager ears
Told how it fared with his sweet mistress there.

(*What follows is to the Music* GONDAKIRÎ *and the Mode*
RUPAKA.)

Krishna! 'tis thou must come, (she sang)
   Ever she waits thee in heavenly bower ;
The lotus seeks not the wandering bee,
   The bee must find the flower.

All the wood over her deep eyes roam,

    Marvelling sore where tarries the bee,

Who leaves such lips of nectar unsought

    As those that blossom for thee.

Her steps would fail if she tried to come,

    Would falter and fail, with yearning weak;

At the first of the road they would falter and pause,

    And the way is strange to seek.

Find her where she is sitting, then,

    With lotus-blossom on ankle and arm

Wearing thine emblems, and musing of nought

    But the meeting to be—glad, warm.

To be—"but wherefore tarrieth he?"

    "What can stay or delay him?—go!

See if the soul of Krishna comes,"

    Ten times she sayeth to me so;

Ten times lost in a languorous swoon,

    " Now he cometh—he cometh," she cries;

And a love-look lightens her eyes in the gloom,

    And the darkness is sweet with her sighs.

Till, watching in vain, she glideth again
    Under the shade of the whispering leaves;
With a heart too full of its love at last
    To heed how her bosom heaves.

> *Shall not these fair verses swell*
> *The number of the wise who dwell*
> *In the realm of Kama's bliss?*
> *Jayadeva prayeth this,*
> *Jayadev, the bard of Love,*
> *Servant of the Gods above.*

For all so strong in Heaven itself
    Is Love, that Radha sits drooping there,
Her beautiful bosoms panting with thought,
    And the braids drawn back from her ear.

And—angel albeit—her rich lips breathe
    Sighs, if sighs were ever so sweet;
And—if spirits can tremble—she trembles now
    From forehead to jewelled feet.

And her voice of music sinks to a sob,
    And her eyes, like eyes of a mated roe,

Are tender with looks of yielded love,
　With dreams dreamed long ago;

Long—long ago, but soon to grow truth,
　To end, and be waking and certain and true;
Of which dear surety murmur her lips,
　As the lips of sleepers do:

And, dreaming, she loosens her girdle-pearls,
　And opens her arms to the empty air,
Then starts, if a leaf of the champâk falls,
　Sighing, "O leaf! is he there?"

Why dost thou linger in this dull spot,
　Haunted by serpents and evil for thee?
Why not hasten to Nanda's House?
　It is plain, if thine eyes could see.

　　May these words of high endeavour—
　　Full of grace and gentle favour—
　　Find out those whose hearts can feel
　　What the message did reveal,

Words that Radha's messenger
Unto Krishna took from her,
Slowly guiding him to come
Through the forest to his home,
Guiding him to find the road
Which led—though long—to Love's abode.

(Here ends that Sarga of the Gîta Govinda entitled
DHRISHTAVAIKUNTO.)

SARGA THE SEVENTH.

—o—

VIPRALABDHAVARNANE NAGARANARAYANO.

KRISHNA SUPPOSED FALSE.

MEANTIME the moon, the rolling moon, clomb high,
And over all Vrindávana it shone;
The moon which on the front of gentle night
Gleams like the chundun-mark on beauty's brow;
The conscious moon which hath its silver face
Marred with the shame of lighting earthly loves:

And while the round white lamp of earth rose higher,
And still he tarried, Radha, petulant,
Sang soft impatience and half-earnest fears:

(*What follows is to the Music* MÂLAVA *and the Mode*
YATI.)

'Tis time!—he comes not!—will he come?
　　Can he leave me thus to pine?
　Yami hê kam sharanam!
　　Ah! what refuge then is mine?

For his sake I sought the wood,
　　Threaded dark and devious ways;
　Yami hê kam sharanam!
　　Can it be Krishna betrays?

Let me die then, and forget
　　Anguish, patience, hope, and fear;
　Yami hê kam sharanam!
　　Ah, why have I held him dear?

Ah, this soft night torments me,
　　Thinking that his faithless arms—
　Yami hê kam sharanam!—
　　Clasp some shadow of my charms.

Fatal shadow—foolish mock!

    When the great love shone confessed ;—

Yami hê kam sharanam !

    Krishna's lotus loads my breast;

'Tis too heavy, lacking him ;

    Like a broken flower I am—

Necklets, jewels, what are ye ?

      Yami hê kam sharanam !

  Yami hê kam sharanam !

    The sky is still, the forest sleeps ;

Krishna forgets—he loves no more ;

    He fails in faith, and Radha weeps.

      But the poet Jayadev—

      He who is great Hari's slave,

      He who finds asylum sweet

      Only at great Hari's feet ;

      He who for your comfort sings

      All this to the Vina's strings—

      Prays that Radha's tender moan

      In your hearts be thought upon,

And that all her holy grace
Live there like the loved one's face.

Yet, if I wrong him! (sang she)—can he fail?
 Could any in the wood win back his kisses?
Could any softest lips of earth prevail
 To hold him from my arms? any love-blisses

Blind him once more to mine?   O Soul, my prize!
 Art thou not merely hindered at this hour?
Sore-wearied, wandering, lost? how otherwise
 Shouldst thou not hasten to the bridal-bower?

But seeing far away that Maiden come
Alone, with eyes cast down and lingering steps,
Again a little while she feared to hear
Of Krishna false; and her quick thoughts took shape
In a fine jealousy, with words like these—

 Something then of earth has held him
  From his home above,
 Some one of those slight deceivers—
  Ah, my foolish love!

Some new face, some winsome playmate,
   With her hair untied,
And the blossoms tangled in it,
   Woos him to her side.

On the dark orbs of her bosom—
   Passionately heaved—
Sink and rise the warm, white pearl-strings,
   Oh, my love deceived !

Fair ? yes, yes ! the rippled shadow
   Of that midnight hair
Shows above her brow—as clouds do
   O'er the moon—most fair :

And she knows, with wilful paces,
   How to make her zone
Gleam and please him ; and her ear-rings
   Tinkle love ; and grown

Coy as he grows fond, she meets him
   With a modest show ;
Shaming truth with truthful seeming,
   While her laugh—light, low—

And her subtle mouth that murmurs,
    And her silken cheek,
And her eyes, say she dissembles
    Plain as speech could speak.

Till at length, a fatal victress,
    Of her triumph vain,
On his neck she lies and smiles there:—
    Ah, my Joy !—my Pain !

But may Radha's fond annoy,
And may Krishna's dawning joy,
Warm and waken love more fit —
Jayadeva prayeth it—
And the griefs and sins assuage
Of this blind and evil age.

O Moon ! (she sang) that art so pure and pale,
    Is Krishna wan like thee with lonely waiting ?
O lamp of love ! art thou the lover's friend,
    And wilt not bring him, my long pain abating ?
O fruitless moon ! thou dost increase my pain
O faithless Krishna ! I have striven in vain.

And then, lost in her fancies sad, she moaned—

What follows is to the Music GURJJARÎ *and the Mode*
EKATÂLÎ.)

In vain, in vain !
Earth will of earth ! I mourn more than I blame ;
   If he had known, he would not sit and paint
The tilka on her smooth black brow, nor claim
   Quick kisses from her yielded lips—false, faint—
False, fragrant, fatal !   Krishna's quest is o'er
      By Jumna's shore !

Vain—it was vain !
The temptress was too near, the heav'n too far ;
   I can but weep because he sits and ties
Garlands of fire-flowers for her loosened hair,
   And in its silken shadow veils his eyes
And buries his fond face.   Yet I forgave
      By Jumna's wave !

Vainly ! all vain !
Make then the most of that whereto thou'rt given,
   Feign her thy Paradise—thy Love of loves ;

E

Say that her eyes are stars, her face the heaven,

   Her bosoms the two worlds, with sandal-groves

Full-scented, and the kiss-marks—ah, thy dream

     By Jumna's stream!

     It shall be vain!

And vain to string the emeralds on her arm,

   And hang the milky pearls upon her neck,

Saying they are not jewels, but a swarm

   Of crowded, glossy bees, come there to suck

The rosebuds of her breast, the sweetest flowers

     Of Jumna's bowers.

     That shall be vain!

Nor wilt thou so believe thine own blind wooing,

   Nor slake thy heart's thirst even with the cup

Which at the last she brims for thee, undoing

   Her girdle of carved gold, and yielding up,

Love's uttermost: brief the poor gain and pride

     By Jumna's tide

     Because still vain

Is love that feeds on shadow; vain, as thou dost,

   To look so deep into the phantom eyes

For that which lives not there; and vain, as thou must,
  To marvel why the painted pleasure flies,
When the fair, false wings seemed folded for ever
      By Jumna's river.

      And vain! yes, vain!
For me too is it, having so much striven,
  To see this slight snare take thee, and thy soul
Which should have climbed to mine, and shared my
      heaven,
  Spent on a lower loveliness, whose whole
Passion of claim were but a parody
      Of that kept here for thee.

      Ahaha! vain!
For on some isle of Jumna's silver stream
  He gives all that they ask to those hard eyes,
While mine which are his angel's, mine which gleam
  With light that might have led him to the skies—
That almost led him—are eclipsed with tears
      Wailing my fruitless prayers.

      But thou, good Friend,
Hang not thy head for shame, nor come so slowly,
  As one whose message is too ill to tell;

If thou must say Krishna is forfeit wholly—
  Wholly forsworn and lost—let the grief dwell
Where the sin doth,—except in this sad heart,
      Which cannot shun its part.

      O great Hari! purge from wrong
      The soul of him who writes this song;
      Purge the souls of those that read
      From every fault of thought and deed;
      With thy blessed light assuage
      The darkness of this evil age!
      Jayadev the bard of love,
      Servant of the Gods above,
      Prays it for himself and you—
      Gentle hearts who listen!—too.

    Then in this other strain she wailed his loss—

  (*What follows is to the Music* DESHAVARÂDÎ *and the*
            Mode RUPAKA.

        She, not Radha, wins the crown
          Whose false lips seemed dearest;

What was distant gain to him
  When sweet loss stood nearest ?
Love her, therefore, lulled to loss
  On her fatal bosom ;
Love her with such love as she
  Can give back in the blossom.

Love her, O thou rash lost soul !
  With thy thousand graces ;
Coin rare thoughts into fair words
  For her face of faces ;
Praise it, fling away for it
  Life's purpose in a sigh,
All for those lips like flower-leaves,
  And lotus-dark deep eye.

Nay, and thou shalt be happy too
  Till the fond dream is over ;
And she shall taste delight to hear
  The wooing of her lover ;
The breeze that brings the sandal up
  From distant green Malay,
Shall seem all fragrance in the night,
  All coolness in the day.

The crescent moon shall seem to swim
　　Only that she may see
The glad eyes of my Krishna gleam,
　　And her soft glances he :
It shall be as a silver lamp
　　Set in the sky to show
The rose-leaf palms that cling and clasp,
　　And the breast that beats below.

The thought of parting shall not lie
　　Cold on their throbbing lives,
The dread of ending shall not chill
　　The glow beginning gives ;
She in her beauty dark shall look—
　　As long as clouds can be—
As gracious as the rain-time cloud
　　Kissing the shining sea.

And he, amid his playmates old,
　　At least a little while,
Shall not breathe forth again the sigh
　　That spoils the song and smile ;

Shall be left wholly to his choice,

    Free for his pleasant sin,

With the golden-girdled damsels

    Of the bowers I found him in.

For me, his Angel, only

    The sorrow and the smart,

The pale grief sitting on the brow,

    The dead hope in the heart;

For me the loss of losing,

    For me the ache and dearth;

My king crowned with the wood-flowers!

    My fairest upon earth!

    Hari, Lord and King of love!

    From thy throne of light above

    Stoop to help us, deign to take

    Our spirits to thee for the sake

    Of this song, which speaks the fears

    Of all who weep with Radha's tears.

But love is strong to pardon, slow to part,

And still the Lady, in her fancies, sang—

Wind of the Indian stream!
A little—oh! a little—breathe once more
The fragrance like his mouth's! blow from thy shore
 One last word as he fades into a dream;

 Bodiless Lord of love!
Show him once more to me a minute's space,
My Krishna, with the love-look in his face,
 And then I come to my own place above;

 I will depart and give
All back to Fate and her: I will submit
To thy stern will, and bow myself to it,
 Enduring still, though desolate, to live:

 If it indeed be life,
Even so resigning, to sit patience-mad,
To feel the zephyrs burn, the sunlight sad,
 The peace of holy heaven, a restless strife.

 Haho! what words are these?
How can I live and lose him? how not go
Whither love draws me for a soul loved so?
 How yet endure such sorrow?—or how cease?

Wind of the Indian wave!
If that thou canst, blow poison here, not nard ;
God of the five shafts! shoot thy sharpest hard,
   And kill me, Radha,—Radha who forgave!

   Or, bitter River,
Yamûn! be Yama's sister! be Death's kin!
Swell thy wave up to me and gulf me in,
   Cooling this cruel, burning pain for ever.

   Ah! if only visions stir
   Grief so passionate in her,
   What divine grief will not take,
   Spirits in heaven for the sake
   Of those who miss love?   Oh, be wise!
   Mark this story of the skies ;
   Meditate Govinda ever,
   Sitting by the sacred river,
   The mystic stream, which o'er his feet
   Glides slow, with murmurs low and sweet,
   Till none can tell whether those be
   Blue lotus-blooms, seen veiledly
   Under the wave, or mirrored gems
   Reflected from the diadems

Bound on the brows of mighty Gods,
Who lean from out their pure abodes,
And leave their bright felicities
To guide great Krishna to his skies.

(*Here ends that Sarga of the Gîta Govinda entitled*
VIPRALABDHAVARNANE NAGARANARAYANO.)

SARGA THE EIGHTH.

—o—

KHANDITAVARNANE
VILAKSHALAKSHMIPATI.

THE REBUKING OF KRISHNA.

For when the weary night had worn away
In these vain fears, and the clear morning broke,
Lo, Krishna! lo, the longed-for of her soul
Came too!—in the glad light he came, and bent
His knee, and clasped his hands; on his dumb lips
Fear, wonder, joy, passion, and reverence
Strove for the trembling words, and Radha knew
Peace won for him and her; yet none the less
A little time she chided him, and sang:

(*What follows is to the Music* BHAIRAVÎ *and the Mode*
YATI.)

Krishna!—then thou hast found me!—and thine eyes
　　Heavy and sad and stained, as if with weeping!
Ah! is it not that those, which were thy prize,
　　So radiant seemed that all night thou wert keeping
Vigils of tender wooing?—have thy Love!
　　Here is no place for vows broken in making;
Thou Lotus-eyed! thou soul for whom I strove!
　　Go! ere I listen, my just mind forsaking.

Krishna! my Krishna with the woodland-wreath!
　　Return, or I shall soften as I blame;
The while thy very lips are dark to the teeth
　　With dye that from her lids and lashes came,
Left on the mouth I touched.　Fair traitor! go!
　　Say not they darkened, lacking food and sleep
Long waiting for my face; I turn it—so—
　　Go! ere I half believe thee, pleading deep;

But wilt thou plead, when, like a love-verse printed
　　On the smooth polish of an emerald,

I see the marks she stamped, the kisses dinted
　Large-lettered, by her lips ? thy speech withheld
Speaks all too plainly; go,—abide thy choice !
　If thou dost stay, I shall more greatly grieve thee;
Not records of her victory ?—peace, dear voice !
　Hence with that godlike brow, lest I believe thee.

For dar'st thou feign the saffron on thy bosom
　Was not implanted in disloyal embrace ?
Or that this many-coloured love-tree blossom
　Shone not, but yesternight, above her face ?
Comest thou here, so late, to be forgiven,
　O thou, in whose eyes Truth was made to live ?
O thou, so worthy else of grace and heaven ?
　O thou, so nearly won ?　Ere I forgive,

Go, Krishna ! go !—lest I should think, unwise,
　Thy heart not false, as thy long lingering seems,
Lest, seeing myself so imaged in thine eyes,
　I shame the name of Pity—turn to dreams
The sacred sound of vows ; make Virtue grudge
　Her praise to Mercy, calling thy sin slight ;

Go therefore, dear offender! go! thy Judge

    Had best not see thee to give sentence right.*

> *But may he grant us peace at last and bliss*
>
> *Who heard,—and smiled to hear,—delays like this,*
>
> *Delays that dallied with a dream come true,*
>
> *Fond wilful angers; for the maid laughed too*
>
> *To see, as Radha ended, her hand take*
>
> *His dark robe for her veil, and Krishna make*
>
> *The word she spoke for parting kindliest sign*
>
> *He should not go, but stay.   O grace divine,*
>
> *Be ours too!   Jayadev, the Poet of love,*
>
> *Prays it from Hari, lordliest above.*

(*Here ends that Sarga of the Gîta Govinda entitled* KHANDITAVARNANE VILAKSHALAKSHMIPATI.)

---

* The text here is not closely followed.

SARGA THE NINTH.

———o———

KALAHANTARITAVARNANE
MUGDHAMUKUNDO.

THE END OF KRISHNA'S TRIAL.

YET not quite did the doubts of Radha die,

Nor her sweet brows unbend; but she, the Maid—

Knowing her heart so tender, her soft arms

Aching to take him in, her rich mouth sad

For the comfort of his kiss, and these fears false—

Spake yet a little in fair words like these :

(*What follows is to the Music* GURJJARÎ *and the Mode*
YATI.)

The lesson that thy faithful love has taught him

He has heard;

The wind of spring, obeying thee, hath brought him

At thy word;

What joy in all the three worlds was so precious
                    To thy mind?
Mâ kooroo mânini mânamayè, *
                    Ah, be kind!

No longer from his earnest eyes conceal
                    Thy delights;
Lift thy face, and let the jealous veil reveal
                    All his rights;
The glory of thy beauty was but given
                    For content;
Mâ kooroo mânini mânamayè,
                    Oh, relent!

Remember, being distant, how he bore thee
                    In his heart;
Look on him sadly turning from before thee
                    To depart;
Is he not the soul thou lovedst, sitting lonely
                    In the wood?
Mâ kooroo mânini mânamayè,
                    'Tis not good!

---

* My proud one! do not indulge in scorn.

He who grants thee high delight in bridal-bower
 Pardons long;
What the gods do love may do at such an hour
 Without wrong;
Why weepest thou? why keepest thou in anger
 Thy lashes down?
Mâ kooroo mânini mânamayè,
 Do not frown!

Lift thine eyes now, and look on him, bestowing,
 Without speech;
Let him pluck at last the flower so sweetly growing
 In his reach;
The fruit of lips, of loving tones, of glances
 That forgive;
Mâ kooroo mânini mânamayè,
 Let him live!

Let him speak with thee, and pray to thee, and prove thee
 All his truth;
Let his silent loving lamentation move thee
 Asking ruth;

F

How knowest thou ?   Ah, listen, dearest Lady,

He is there ;

Mâ kooroo mânini mânamayè,

Thou must hear !

O rare voice, which is a spell

Unto all on earth who dwell !

O rich voice of rapturous love,

Making melody above !

Krishna's, Hari's—one in two,

Sound these mortal verses through !

Sound like that soft flute which made

Such a magic in the shade—

Calling deer-eyed maidens nigh,

Waking wish and stirring sigh,

Thrilling blood and melting breasts,

Whispering love's divine unrests,

Winning blessings to descend,

Bringing earthly ills to end ;—

Be thou heard in this song now

Thou, the great Enchantment, thou !

(*Here ends that Sarga of the Gîta Govinda entitled* KALAHANTARITAVARNANE MUGDHAMUKUNDO.)

SARGA THE TENTH.

———o———

MANINIVARNANE
CHATURACHATURBHUJO.

KRISHNA IN PARADISE.

BUT she, abasing still her glorious eyes,
And still not yielding all her face to him,
Relented; till with softer upturned look
She smiled, while the Maid pleaded; so thereat
Came Krishna nearer, and his eager lips
Mixed sighs with words in this fond song he sang:

(*What follows is to the Music* DESHÎYAVARÂDÎ *and the*
Mode ASHTATÂLÎ.)

O angel of my hope! O my heart's home!
My fear is lost in love, my love in fear;

This bids me trust my burning wish, and come,
 That checks me with its memories, drawing near:
Lift up thy look, and let the thing it saith
End fear with grace, or darken love to death.

Or only speak once more, for though thou slay me,
 Thy heavenly mouth must move, and I shall hear
Dulcet delights of perfect music sway me
 Again—again that voice so blest and dear;
Sweet Judge! the prisoner prayeth for his doom
That he may hear his fate divinely come.

Speak once more! then thou canst not choose but show
 Thy mouth's unparalleled and honeyed wonder
Where, like pearls hid in red-lipped shells, the row
 Of pearly teeth thy rose-red lips lie under;
Ah me! I am that bird that woos the moon,
And pipes—poor fool! to make it glitter soon.

Yet hear me on—because I cannot stay
 The passion of my soul, because my gladness
Will pour forth from my heart;—since that far day
 When through the mist of all my sin and sadness

Thou didst vouchsafe—Surpassing One!—to break,
All else I slighted for thy noblest sake.

Thou, thou hast been my blood, my breath, my being;
  The pearl to plunge for in the sea of life;
The sight to strain for, past the bounds of seeing;
  The victory to win through longest strife;
My Queen! my crownèd Mistress! my sphered bride!
Take this for truth, that what I say beside

Of bold love—grown full-orbed at sight of thee—
  May be forgiven with a quick remission;
For, thou divine fulfilment of all hope!
  Thou all-undreamed completion of the vision!
I gaze upon thy beauty, and my fear
Passes as clouds do, when the moon shines clear.

So if thou'rt angry still, this shall avail,
  Look straight at me, and let thy bright glance wound
    me;
Fetter me! gyve me! lock me in the gaol
  Of thy delicious arms; make fast around me
The silk-soft manacles of wrists and hands,
Then kill me! I shall never break those bands.

The starlight jewels flashing on thy breast

    Have not my right to hear thy beating heart;

The happy jasmine-buds that clasp thy waist

    Are soft usurpers of my place and part;

If that fair girdle only there must shine,

Give me the girdle's life—the girdle mine!

Thy brow like smooth Bandhûka-leaves; thy cheek

    Which the dark-tinted Madhuk's velvet shows;

Thy long-lashed Lotus eyes, lustrous and meek;

    Thy nose a Tila-bud; thy teeth like rows

Of Kunda-petals! he who pierceth hearts

Points with thy lovelinesses all five darts.

But Radiant, Perfect, Sweet, Supreme, forgive!

    My heart is wise—my tongue is foolish still:

I know where I am come—I know I live—

    I know that thou art Radha—that this will

Last and be heaven: that I have leave to rise

Up from thy feet, and look into thine eyes!

    And, nearer coming, I ask for grace

        Now that the blest eyes turn to mine;

Faithful I stand in this sacred place
    Since first I saw them shine :
Dearest glory that stills my voice,
    Beauty unseen, unknown, unthought!
Splendour of love, in whose sweet light
    Darkness is past and nought;
Ah, beyond words that sound on earth,
    Golden bloom of the garden of heaven!
Radha, enchantress! Radha, the queen!
    Be this trespass forgiven—
In that I dare, with courage too much
    And a heart afraid,—so bold it is grown—
To hold thy hand with a bridegroom's touch,
    And take thee for mine, mine own.*

        So they met and so they ended
        Pain and parting, being blended
        Life with life—made one for ever
        In high love; and Jayadeva
        Hasteneth on to close the story
        Of their bridal grace and glory.

(Here ends that Sarga of the Gîta Govinda entitled
MANINIVARNANE CHATURACHATURBHUJO.)

---

* Much here also is necessarily paraphrased.

SARGA THE ELEVENTH.

———o———

RADHIKAMILANE
SANANDADAMODARO.

THE UNION OF RADHA AND KRISHNA.

THUS followed soft and lasting peace, and griefs
Died while she listened to his tender tongue,
Her eyes of antelope alight with love;
And while he led the way to the bride-bower
The maidens of her train adorned her fair
With golden marriage-cloths, and sang this song:

(*What follows is to the Music* VASANTA *and the Mode*
YATI.)

Follow, happy Radha! follow,—
In the quiet falling twilight—

The steps of him who followed thee
  So steadfastly and far;
Let us bring thee where the banjulas
  Have spread a roof of crimson,
Lit up by many a marriage-lamp
  Of planet, sun, and star:
For the hours of doubt are over,
  And thy glad and faithful lover
Hath found the road by tears and prayers
  To thy divinest side;
And thou wilt not now deny him
  One delight of all thy beauty,
But yield up open-hearted
  His pearl, his prize, his bride.

Oh, follow! while we fill the air
  With songs and softest music;
Lauding thy wedded loveliness,
  Dear Mistress past compare!
For there is not any splendour
  Of Apsarasas immortal—
No glory of their beauty rich—
  But Radha has a share;

Oh, follow ! while we sing the song
   That fills the worlds with longing,
The music of the Lord of love
   Who melts all hearts with bliss;
For now is born the gladness
   That springs from mortal sadness,
And all soft thoughts and things and hopes
   Were presages of this.

Then, follow, happiest Lady !
   Follow him thou lovest wholly;
The hour is come to follow now
   The soul thy spells have led;
His are thy breasts like jasper-cups,
   And his thine eyes like planets;
Thy fragrant hair, thy stately neck,
   Thy queenly sumptuous head;
Thy soft small feet, thy perfect lips,
   Thy teeth like jasmine petals,
Thy gleaming rounded shoulders,
   And long caressing arms,
Being thine to give, are his; and his
   The twin strings of thy girdle,

And his the priceless treasure
  Of thine utter-sweetest charms.

So follow! while the flowers break forth
  In white and amber clusters,
At the breath of thy pure presence,
  And the radiance on thy brow;
Oh, follow where the Asokas wave
  Their sprays of gold and purple,
As if to beckon thee the way
  That Krishna passed but now;
He is gone a little forward!
  Though thy steps are faint for pleasure,
Let him hear the tattling ripple
  Of the bangles round thy feet;
Moving slowly o'er the blossoms
  On the path which he has shown thee,
That when he turns to listen
  It may make his fond heart beat.

And loose thy jewelled girdle
  A little, that its rubies
May tinkle softest music too,
  And whisper thou art near;

Though now, if in the forest
   Thou should'st bend one blade of Kusha
With silken touch of passing foot,
   His heart would know and hear;
Would hear the wood-buds saying,
   " It is Radha's foot that passes;"
Would hear the wind sigh love-sick,
   " It is Radha's fragrance, this;"
Would hear thine own heart beating
   Within thy panting bosom,
And know thee coming, coming,
   His—ever,—ever—his!

" *Mine!* "—hark! we are near enough for hearing—
   " *Soon she will come—she will smile—she will say*
Honey-sweet words of heavenly endearing;
   O soul! listen; my Bride is on her way! "

Hear'st him not, my Radha?
   Lo, night bendeth o'er thee—
Darker than dark Tamâla-leaves—
   To list thy marriage-song;
Dark as the touchstone that tries gold,
   And see now—on before thee—

Those lines of tender light that creep
  The clouded sky along:
O night! that trieth gold of love,
  This love is proven perfect!
O lines that streak the touchstone sky,
  Flash forth true shining gold!
O rose-leaf feet, go boldly!
  O night!—that lovest lovers—
Thy softest robe of silence
  About these bridals fold!

See'st thou not, my Radha?
  Lo, the night, thy bridesmaid,
Comes!—her eyes thick-painted
  With soorma of the gloom—
The night that binds the planet-worlds
  For jewels on her forehead,
And for emblem and for garland
  Loves the blue-black lotus-bloom;
The night that scents her breath so sweet
  With cool and musky odours,
That joys to spread her veil of shade
  Over the limbs of love;

And when, with loving weary,

    Yet dreaming love, they slumber,

Sets the far stars for silver lamps

    To light them from above.

So came she where he stood, awaiting her

At the bower's entry, like a god to see,

With marriage-gladness and the grace of heaven.

The great pearl set upon his glorious head

Shone like a moon among the leaves, and shone

Like stars the gems that kept her gold gown close :

But still a little while she paused—abashed

At her delight, of her deep joy afraid—

And they that tended her sang once more this :

(*What follows is to the Music* VARÂDI *and the Mode*
        RUPAKA.)

Enter, thrice-happy ! enter, thrice-desired !

And let the gates of Hari shut thee in

With the soul destined to thee from of old.

Tremble not ! lay thy lovely shame aside ;

Lay it aside with thine unfastened zone,

And love him with the love that knows not fear,

Because it fears not change; enter thou in,
Flower of all sweet and stainless womanhood!
For ever to grow bright, for ever new;

Enter beneath the flowers, O flower-fair!
Beneath these tendrils, Loveliest! that entwine
And clasp, and wreathe and cling, with kissing stems;

Enter, with tender-blowing airs of heaven,
Soft as love's breath and gentle as the tones
Of lover's whispers, when the lips come close:

Enter the house of Love, O loveliest!
Enter the marriage-bower, most beautiful!
And take and give the joy that Hari grants.

Thy heart has entered, let thy feet go too!
Lo, Krishna! lo, the one that thirsts for thee!
Give him the drink of amrit from thy lips.

————

Then she, no more delaying, entered straight;
Her step a little faltered, but her face
Shone with unutterable quick love; and—while

The music of her bangles passed the porch—
Shame, which had lingered in her downcast eyes,
Departed shamed* . . . and like the mighty deep,
Which sees the moon and rises, all his life
Uprose to drink her beams.

(*Here ends that Sarga of the Gîta Govinda entitled*
Radhikamilane Sanandadamodaro.)

———

Hari keep you!   He whose might,
     On the King of Serpents seated,
Flashes forth in dazzling light
     From the Great Snake's gems repeated:
Hari keep you!   He whose graces,
     Manifold in majesty,—
Multiplied in heavenly places—
     Multiply on earth—to see

———

* This complete anticipation (*salajjâ lajjâpi*) of the line—
     " Upon whose brow shame is ashamed to sit"
—occurs at the close of the Sarga, part of which is here perforce
omitted, along with the whole of the last one.

Better with a hundred eyes
  Her bright charms who by him lies.

———————

What skill may be in singing,
  What worship sound in song,
What lore be taught in loving,
  What right divined from wrong:
Such things hath Jayadeva—
  In this his Hymn of Love,
Which lauds Govinda ever,—
  Displayed ; may all approve !

THE END OF THE INDIAN SONG OF SONGS.

G

MISCELLANEOUS ORIENTAL POEMS.

THE RAJPOOT WIFE.

————o————

SING something, Jymul Rao! for the goats are gathered
    now,
  And no more water is to bring;
The village-gates are set, and the night is gray as yet,
  God hath given wondrous fancies to thee:—sing!

Then Jymul's supple fingers, with a touch that doubts
    and lingers,
  Sets athrill the saddest wire of all the six;
And the girls sit in a tangle, and hush the tinkling bangle,
  While the boys pile the flame with store of sticks.

And vain of village praise, but full of ancient days,
  He begins with a smile and with a sigh—
" Who knows the babul-tree by the bend of the Ravee ?"
  Quoth Gunesh, " I!" and twenty voices, " I!"

"Well—listen! there below, in the shade of bloom and
  bough,
  Is a musjid of carved and coloured stone;
And Abdool Shureef Khan—I spit, to name that man!—
  Lieth there, underneath, all alone.

"He was Sultan Mahmood's vassal, and wore an Amir's
  tassel
  In his green hadj-turban, at Nungul.
Yet the head which went so proud, it is not in his shroud;
  There are bones in that grave,—but not a skull!

"And, deep drove in his breast, there moulders with the
  rest
  A dagger, brighter once than Chundra's ray;
A Rajpoot lohar whet it, and a Rajpoot woman set it
  Past the power of any hand to tear away.

"'Twas the Ranee Neila true, the wife of Soorj Dehu,
  Lord of the Rajpoots of Nourpoor;
You shall hear the mournful story, with its sorrow and
  its glory,
  And curse Shureef Khan,—the soor!"

All in the wide Five-Waters was none like Soorj Dehu,
To foeman who so dreadful, to friend what heart so true?

Like Indus, through the mountains came down the
    Muslim ranks,
And town-walls fell before them as flooded river-banks;

But Soorj Dehu the Rajpoot owned neither town nor
    wall;
His house the camp, his roof-tree the sky that covers all;

His seat of state the saddle; his robe a shirt of mail;
His court a thousand Rajpoots close at his stallion's tail.

Not less was Soorj a Rajah because no crown he wore
Save the grim helm of iron with sword-marks dinted
    o'er;

Because he grasped no sceptre save the sharp tulwar,
    made
Of steel that fell from heaven,—for 'twas Indra forged
    that blade!

And many a starless midnight the shout of " Soorj Dehu "
Broke up with spear and matchlock the Muslim's
  "Illahu."

And many a day of battle upon the Muslim proud
Fell Soorj, as Indra's lightning falls from the silent cloud.

Nor ever shot nor arrow, nor spear nor slinger's stone,
Could pierce the mail that Neila the Ranee buckled on :

But traitor's subtle tongue-thrust through fence of steel
  can break ;
And Soorj was taken sleeping, whom none had ta'en
  awake.

Then at the noon, in durbar, swore fiercely Shureef Khan
That Soorj should die in torment, or live a Mussulman.

But Soorj laughed lightly at him, and answered, " Work
  your will !
The last breath of my body shall curse your Prophet still."

With words of insult shameful, and deeds of cruel kind,
They vexed that Rajpoot's body, but never moved his
  mind.

And one is come who sayeth, "Ho! Rajpoots! Soorj is
   bound;
Your lord is caged and baited by Shureef Khan, the
   hound.

"The Khan hath caught and chained him, like a beast,
   in iron cage,
And all the camp of Islam spends on him spite and
   rage;

"All day the coward Muslims spend on him rage and
   spite;
If ye have thought to help him, 'twere good ye go to-
   night."

Up sprang a hundred horsemen, flashed in each hand a
   sword;
In each heart burned the gladness of dying for their
   lord;

Up rose each Rajpoot rider, and buckled on with speed
The bridle-chain and breast-cord, and the saddle of his
   steed.

But unto none sad Neila gave word to mount and ride;
Only she called the brothers of Soorj unto her side,

And said, "Take order straightway to seek this camp
  with me;
If love and craft can conquer, a thousand is as three.

"If love be weak to save him, Soorj dies—and ye
  return,
For where a Rajpoot dieth, the Rajpoot widows burn."

Thereat the Ranee Neila unbraided from her hair
The pearls as great as Kashmir grapes Soorj gave his
  wife to wear,

And all across her bosoms—like lotus-buds to see—
She wrapped the tinselled sari of a dancing Kunchenee;

And fastened on her ankles the hundred silver bells,
To whose light laugh of music the Nautch-girl darts and
  dwells.

And all in dress a Nautch-girl, but all in heart a queen,
She set her foot to stirrup with a sad and settled mien.

Only one thing she carried no Kunchenee should bear,
The knife between her bosoms;—ho, Shureef! have a
   care!
   _____

Thereat, with running ditty of mingled pride and pity,
   Jymul Rao makes the six wires sigh;
And the girls with tearful eyes note the music's fall
      and rise,
   And the boys let the fire fade and die.

   _____

All day lay Soorj the Rajpoot in Shureef's iron cage,
All day the coward Muslims spent on him spite and
   rage.

With bitter cruel torments, and deeds of shameful kind,
They racked and broke his body, but could not shake
      his mind.

And only at the Azan, when all their worst was vain,
They left him, like dogs slinking from a lion in his pain.

No meat nor drink they gave him through all that
      burning day,
And done to death, but scornful, at twilight-time he lay.

So when the gem of Shiva uprose, the shining moon,
Soorj spake unto his spirit, "The end is coming soon.

"I would the end might hasten, could Neila only know—
What is that Nautch-girl singing with voice so known
    and low?

"Singing beneath the cage-bars the song of love and fear
My Neila sang at parting!—what doth that Nautch-girl
    here?

"Whence comes she by the music of Neila's tender
    strain,
She, in that shameless tinsel?—O Nautch-girl, sing
    again!"

"Ah, Soorj!"—so followed answer—"here thine own
    Neila stands,
Faithful in life and death alike,—look up, and take my
    hands:

"Speak low, lest the guard hear us;—to-night, if thou
    must die,
Shureef shall have no triumph, but bear thee company."

So sang she like the Koïl that dies beside its mate ;
With eye as black and fearless, and love as hot and great.

Then the Chief laid his pale lips upon the little palm,
And sank down with a smile of love, his face all glad
and calm ;

And through the cage-bars Neila felt the brave heart
stop fast,
"O Soorj !"—she cried—"I follow ! have patience to
the last."

She turned and went. "Who passes?" challenged the
Mussulman ;
"A Nautch-girl, I."—"What seek'st thou ?"—"The
presence of the Khan ;

"Ask if the high chief-captain be pleased to hear me
sing ;"
And Shureef, full of feasting, the Kunchenee bade bring.

Then, all before the Muslims, aflame with lawless wine,
Entered the Ranee Neila, in grace and face divine ;

And all before the Muslims, wagging their goatish chins,
The Rajpoot Princess set her to the "bee-dance" that
    begins,

    " If my love loved me, he should be a bee,
      I the yellow champak, love the honey of me."

All the wreathëd movements danced she of that dance;
Not a step she slighted, not a wanton glance;

In her unveiled bosom chased th' intruding bee,
To her waist—and lower—she! a Rajpoot, she!

Sang the melting music, swayed the languorous limb:
Shureef's drunken heart beat—Shureef's eyes waxed
    dim.

From his finger Shureef loosed an Ormuz pearl—
" By the Prophet," quoth he, " 'tis a winsome girl!

" Take this ring; and 'prithee, come and have thy pay,
I would hear at leisure more of such a lay."

Glared his eyes on her eyes, passing o'er the plain,
Glared at the tent-purdah—never glared again!

Never opened after unto gaze or glance,
Eyes that saw a Rajpoot dance a shameful dance;

For the kiss she gave him was his first and last—
Kiss of dagger, driven to his heart, and past.

At her feet he wallowed, choked with wicked blood;
In his breast the katar quivered where it stood.

At the hilt his fingers vainly—wildly—try,
Then they stiffen feeble;—die! thou slayer, die!

From his jewelled scabbard drew she Shureef's sword,
Cut atwain the neck-bone of the Muslim lord.

Underneath the starlight,—sooth, a sight of dread!
Like the Goddess Kali, comes she with the head,

Comes to where her brothers guard their murdered chief;
All the camp is silent, but the night is brief.

At his feet she flings it, flings her burden vile;
" Soorj! I keep my promise! Brothers, build the pile!"

They have built it, set it, all as Rajpoots do,
From the cage of iron taken Soorj Dehu;

In the lap of Neila, seated on the pile,
Laid his head—she radiant, like a queen the while.

Then the lamp is lighted, and the ghee is poured—
"Soorj, we burn together: O my love, my lord!"

In the flame and crackle dies her tender tongue,
Dies the Ranee, truest, all true wives among.

At the dawn a clamour runs from tent to tent,
Like the wild geese cackling when the night is spent.

"Shureef Khan lies headless! gone is Soorj Dehu!
And the wandering Nautch-girl, who has seen her, who?"

This but know the sentries, at the "breath of morn"
Forth there fared two horsemen, by the first was borne

The urn of clay, the vessel that Rajpoots use to bring
The ashes of dead kinsmen to Gungas' holy spring.

————

KING SALADIN.

——o——

LONG years ago—so tells Boccaccio
In such Italian gentleness of speech
As finds no echo in this northern air
To counterpart its music—long ago,
When Saladin was Soldan of the East,
The kings let cry a general crusade;
And to the trysting-plains of Lombardy
The idle lances of the North and West
Rode all that spring, as all the spring runs down
Into a lake, from all its hanging hills,
The clash and glitter of a hundred streams.

Whereof the rumour reached to Saladin;
And that swart king—as royal in his heart
As any crownèd champion of the Cross—
That he might fully, of his knowledge, learn
The purpose of the lords of Christendom,

H

And when their war and what their armament,

Took thought to cross the seas to Lombardy.

Wherefore, with wise and trustful Amirs twain,

All habited in garbs that merchants use,

With trader's band and gipsire on the breasts

That best loved mail and dagger, Saladin

Set forth upon his journey perilous.

   In that day, lordly land was Lombardy!

A sea of country-plenty, islanded

With cities rich; nor richer one than thee,

Marble Milano! from whose gate at dawn—

With ear that little recked the matin-bell,

But a keen eye to measure wall and foss—

The Soldan rode; and all day long he rode

For Pavia; passing basilic, and shrine,

And gaze of vineyard-workers, wotting not

Yon trader was the Lord of Heathenesse.

All day he rode; yet at the wane of day

No gleam of gate, or ramp, or rising spire,

Nor Tessin's sparkle underneath the stars

Promised him Pavia; but he was 'ware

Of a gay company upon the way,

Ladies and lords, with horses, hawks, and hounds;

Cap-plumes and tresses fluttered by the wind
Of merry race for home. "Go!" said the king
To one that rode upon his better hand,
"And pray these gentles of their courtesy
How many leagues to Pavia, and the gates
What hour they close them?" Then the Saracen
Set spur, and being joined to him that seemed
First of the hunt, he told the message—they
Checking the jangling bits, and chiding down
The unfinished laugh to listen—but by this
Came up the king, his bonnet in his hand,
Theirs doffed to him: "Sir Trader," Torel said
(Messer Torello 'twas, of Istria),
"They shut the Pavian gate at even-song,
And even-song is sung." Then turning half,
Muttered, "Pardie, the man is worshipful,
A stranger too!" "Fair lord!" quoth Saladin,
"Please you to stead some weary travellers,
Saying where we may lodge, the town so far
And night so near." "Of my heart, willingly,"
Made answer Torel, "I did think but now
To send my knave an errand—he shall ride
And bring you into lodgment—oh! no thanks,

Our Lady keep you!" then with whispered hest
He called their guide and sped them.   Being gone,
Torello told his purpose, and the band,
With ready zeal and loosened bridle-chains,
Rode for his hunting-palace, where they set
A goodly banquet underneath the planes,
And hung the house with guest-lights, and anon
Welcomed the wondering strangers, thereto led
Unwitting, by a world of winding paths;
Messer Torello, at the inner gate,
Waiting to take them in—a goodly host,
Stamped current with God's image for a man
Chief among men, truthful, and just, and free.

 Then he, " Well met again, fair sirs !   Our knave
Hath found you shelter better than the worst:
Please you to leave your selles, and being bathed,
Grace our poor supper here."   Then Saladin,
Whose sword had yielded ere his courtesy,
Answered, " Great thanks, Sir Knight, and this much
          blame,
You spoil us for our trade ! two bonnets doffed,
And travellers' questions holding you afield,
For those you give us this."   " Sir ! not your meed,

Nor worthy of your breeding; but in sooth
That is not out of Pavia." Thereupon
He led them to fair chambers decked with all
Makes tired men glad; lights, and the marble bath,
And flasks that sparkled, liquid amethyst,
And grapes, not dry as yet from evening dew.

   Thereafter at the supper-board they sat;
Nor lacked it, though its guest was reared a king,
Worthy provend in crafts of cookery,
Pastel, pasticcio—all set forth on gold;
And gracious talk and pleasant courtesies,
Spoken in stately Latin, cheated time
Till there was none but held the stranger-sir,
For all his chapman's dress of cramasie,
Goodlier than silks could make him. Presently
Talk rose upon the Holy Sepulchre:
"I go myself," said Torel, "with a score
Of better knights—the flower of Pavia—
To try our steel against King Saladin's.
Sirs! ye have seen the countries of the Sun,
Know you the Soldan?" Answer gave the king,
"The Soldan we have seen—'twill push him hard
If, which I nothing doubt, you Pavian lords

Are valorous as gentle;—we, alas!
Are Cyprus merchants making trade to France—
Dull sons of Peace." "By Mary!" Torel cried,
" But for thy word, I ne'er heard speech so fit
To lead the war, nor saw a hand that sat
Liker a soldier's in the sabre's place;
But sure I hold you sleepless!" Then himself
Playing the chamberlain, with torches borne,
Led them to restful beds, commending them
To sleep and God, Who hears—Allah or God—
When good men do his creatures charities.

   At dawn the cock, and neigh of saddled steeds,
Broke the king's dreams of battle—not their own,
But goodly jennets from Torello's stalls,
Caparisoned to bear them; he their host
Up, with a gracious radiance like the sun,
To bid them speed.   Beside him in the court
Stood Dame Adalieta; comely she,
And of her port as queenly, and serene
As if the braided gold about her brows
Had been a crown.   Mutual good-morrow given,
Thanks said and stayed, the lady prayed her guest
To take a token of his sojourn there,

Marking her good-will, not his worthiness;

" A gown of miniver—these furbelows

Are silk I spun—my lord wears ever such—

A housewife's gift! but those ye love are far;

Wear it as given for them."   Then Saladin—

" A precious gift, Madonna, past my thanks;

And—but thou shalt not hear a ' no' from me—

Past my receiving; yet I take it; we

Were debtors to your noble courtesy

Out of redemption—this but bankrupts us."

" Nay, sir,—God shield you ! " said the knight and dame.

And Saladin, with phrase of gentilesse

Returned, or ever that he rode alone,

Swore a great oath in guttural Arabic,

An oath by Allah—startling up the ears

Of those three Christian cattle they bestrode—

That never yet was princelier-natured man,

Nor gentler lady;—and that time should see

For a king's lodging quittance royal repaid.

It was the day of the Passaggio:

Ashore the war-steeds champed the burnished bit;

Afloat the galleys tugged the mooring-chain:
The town was out; the Lombard armourers—
Red-hot with riveting the helmets up,
And whetting axes for the heathen heads—
Cooled in the crowd that filled the squares and streets
To speed God's soldiers.　At the none that day
Messer Torello to the gate came down,
Leading his lady;—sorrow's hueless rose
Grew on her cheek, and thrice the destrier
Struck fire, impatient, from the pavement-squares,
Or ere she spoke, tears in her lifted eyes,
"Goest thou, lord of mine?"　"Madonna, yes!"
Said Torel, "for my soul's weal and the Lord
Ride I to-day: my good name and my house
Reliant I intrust thee, and—because
It may be they shall slay me, and because,
Being so young, so fair, and so reputed,
The noblest will entreat thee—wait for me,
Widow or wife, a year, and month, and day;
Then if thy kinsmen press thee to a choice,
And if I be not come, hold me for dead;
Nor link thy blooming beauty with the grave
Against thine heart."　"Good my lord!" answered she,

" Hardly my heart sustains to let thee go ;

Thy memory it can keep, and keep it will,

Though my one lord, Torel of Istria,

Live, or ——" " Sweet, comfort thee ! San Pietro

      speed!

I shall come home : if not, and worthy knees

Bend for this hand, whereof none worthy lives,

Least he who lays his last kiss thus upon it,

Look thee, I free it ——" " Nay !" she said, " but I,

A petulant slave that hugs her golden chain,

Give that gift back, and with it this poor ring :

Set it upon thy sword-hand, and in fight

Be merciful and win, thinking of me."

Then she, with pretty action, drawing on

Her ruby, buckled over it his glove—

The great steel glove—and through the helmet bars

Took her last kiss ;—then let the chafing steed

Have its hot will and go.

              But Saladin,

Safe back among his lords at Lebanon,

Well wotting of their quest, awaited it,

And held the Crescent up against the Cross.

In many a doughty fight Ferrara blades

Clashed with keen Damasc, many a weary month
Wasted afield; but yet the Christians
Won nothing nearer to Christ's sepulchre;
Nay, but gave ground.   At last, in Acre pent,
On their loose files, enfeebled by the war,
Came stronger smiter than the Saracen—
The deadly Pest: day after day they died,
Pikeman and knight-at-arms; day after day
A thinner line upon the leaguered wall
Held off the heathen:—held them off a space;
Then, over-weakened, yielded, and gave up
The city and the stricken garrison.

  So to sad chains and hateful servitude
Fell all those purple lords—Christendom's stars,
Once high in hope as soaring Lucifer,
Now low as sinking Hesper: with them fell
Messer Torello—never one so poor
Of all the hundreds that his bounty fed
As he in prison—ill-entreated, bound,
Starved of sweet light, and set to shameful tasks;
And that great load at heart to know the days
Fast flying, and to live accounted dead.
One joy his gaolers left him,—his good hawk;

The brave, gay bird that crossed the seas with him:
And often, in the mindful hour of eve,
With tameless eye and spirit masterful,
In a feigned anger checking at his hand,
The good gray falcon made his master cheer.

One day it chanced Saladin rode afield
With shawled and turbaned Amirs, and his hawks—
Lebanon-bred, and mewed as princes lodge—
Flew foul, forgot their feather, hung at wrist,
And slighted call.   The Soldan, quick in wrath,
Bade slay the cravens, scourge the falconer,
And seek some wight who knew the heart of hawks,
To keep it hot and true.   Then spake a Sheikh—
" There is a Frank in prison by the sea,
Far-seen herein."   " Give word that he be brought,"
Quoth Saladin, " and bid him set a cast :
If he hath skill, it shall go well for him."

Thus by the winding path of circumstance
One palace held, as prisoner and prince,
Torello and his guest : unwitting each,
Nay and unwitting, though they met and spake

Of that goshawk and this—signors in serge,

And chapmen crowned, who knows?—till on a time

Some trick of face, the manner of some smile,

Some gleam of sunset from the glad day gone,

Caught the king's eye, and held it. "Nazarene!

What native art thou?" asked he. "Lombard I,

A man of Pavia." "And thy name?" "Torel,

Messer Torello called in happier times,

Now best uncalled." "Come hither, Christian!"

The Soldan said, and led the way, by court

And hall and fountain, to an inner room

Rich with king's robes: therefrom he reached a gown,

And "Know'st thou this?" he asked. "High lord! I

      might

Elsewhere," quoth Torel, "here 'twere mad to say

Yon gown my wife unto a trader gave

Who shared our board." "Nay, but that gown is this,

And she the giver, and the trader I,"

Quoth Saladin; "I! twice a king to-day,

Owing a royal debt and paying it."

Then Torel, sore amazed, "Great lord, I blush,

Remembering how the Master of the East

Lodged sorrily." "It's Master's Master thou!"

Gave answer Saladin, " come in and see
What wares the Cyprus traders keep at home ;
Come forth and take thy place, Saladin's friend."
Therewith into the circle of his lords,
With gracious mien the Soldan led his slave ;
And while the dark eyes glittered, seated him
First of the full divan. " Orient lords,"
So spake he,—" let the one who loves his king
Honour this Frank, whose house sheltered your king ;
He is my brother :" then the night-black beards
Swept the stone floor in ready reverence,
Agas and Amirs welcoming Torel :
And a great feast was set, the Soldan's friend
Royally garbed, upon the Soldan's hand,
Shining the bright star of the banqueters.

All which, and the abounding grace and love
Shown him by Saladin, a little held
The heart of Torel from its Lombard home
With Dame Adalieta : but it chanced
He sat beside the king in audience,
And there came one who said, " Oh, Lord of lords,

That galley of the Genovese which sailed
With Frankish prisoners is gone down at sea."
"Gone down!" cried Torel.   "Ay! what recks it,
          friend,
To fall thy visage for?" quoth Saladin;
"One galley less to ship-stuffed Genoa!"
"Good my liege!" Torel said, "it bore a scroll
Inscribed to Pavia, saying that I lived;
For in a year, a month, and day, not come,
I bade them hold me dead; and dead I am,
Albeit living, if my lady wed,
Perchance constrained."   "Certes," spake Saladin,
"A noble dame—the like not won, once lost—
How many days remain?"   "Ten days, my prince,
And twelvescore leagues between my heart and me:
Alas! how to be passed?"   Then Saladin—
"Lo! I am loath to lose thee—wilt thou swear
To come again if all go well with thee,
Or come ill speeding?"   "Yea, I swear, my king,
Out of true love," quoth Torel, "heartfully."
Then Saladin, "Take here my signet-seal;
My admiral will loose his swiftest sail
Upon its sight; and cleave the seas, and go

And clip thy dame, and say the Trader sends

A gift, remindful of her courtesies."

   Passed were the year, and month, and day ; and passed

Out of all hearts but one Sir Torel's name,

Long given for dead by ransomed Pavians :

For Pavia, thoughtless of her Eastern graves,

A lovely widow, much too gay for grief,

Made peals from half a hundred campaniles

To ring a wedding in. The seven bells

Of Santo Pietro, from the nones to noon,

Boomed with bronze throats the happy tidings out ;

Till the great tenor, overswelled with sound,

Cracked itself dumb. Thereat the sacristan,

Leading his swinkèd ringers down the stairs,

Came blinking into sunlight—all his keys

Jingling their little peal about his belt—

Whom, as he tarried, locking up the porch,

A foreign signor, browned with southern suns,

Turbaned and slippered, as the Muslims use,

Plucked by the cope. "Friend," quoth he—'twas a

     tongue

Italian true, but in a Muslim mouth—

" Why are your belfries busy—is it peace

Or victory, that so ye din the ears
Of Pavian lieges ? "   " Truly, no liege thou ! "
Grunted the sacristan, " who knowest not
That Dame Adalieta weds to-night
Her fore-betrothed,—Sir Torel's widow she,
That died i' the chain ? "   " To-night ! " the stranger said.
" Ay, sir, to-night !—why not to-night ?—to-night !
And you shall see a goodly Christian feast
If so you pass their gates at even-song,
For all are asked."

    No more the questioner,
But folded o'er his face the Eastern hood,
Lest idle eyes should mark how idle words
Had struck him home.   " So quite forgot !—so soon !—
And this the square wherein I gave the joust,
And that the loggia, where I fed the poor ;
And yon my palace, where—oh, fair ! oh, false !—
They robe her for a bridal.   Can it be ?
Clean out of heart, with twice six flying moons,
The heart that beat on mine as it would break,
That faltered forty oaths.   Forced ! forced !—not false—
Well ! I will sit, wife, at thy wedding-feast,
And let mine eyes give my fond faith the lie."

So in the stream of gallant guests that flowed

Feastward at eve, went Torel; passed with them

The outer gates, crossed the great courts with them,

A stranger in the walls that called him lord.

Cressets and coloured lamps made the way bright,

And rose-leaves strewed to where within the doors

The master of the feast, the bridegroom, stood,

A-glitter from his forehead to his foot,

Speaking fair welcomes.   He, a courtly lord,

Marking the Eastern guest, bespoke him sweet,

Prayed place for him, and bade them set his seat

Upon the dais.   Then the feast began,

And wine went free as wit, and music died—

Outdone by merrier laughter:—only one

Nor ate nor drank, nor spoke nor smiled; but gazed

On the pale bride, pale as her crown of pearls,

Who sate so cold and still, and sad of cheer,

At the bride-feast.

                But of a truth, Torel

Read the thoughts right that held her eyelids down,

And knew her loyal to her memories.

Then to a little page who bore the wine,

He spake, " Go tell thy lady thus from me:

                    I

In mine own land, if any stranger sit

A wedding-guest, the bride, out of her grace,

In token that she knows her guest's good-will,

In token she repays it, brims a cup,

Wherefrom he drinking she in turn doth drink;

So is our use."   The little page made speed

And told the message.   Then that lady pale—

Ever a gentle and a courteous heart—

Lifted her troubled eyes and smiled consent

On the swart stranger.   By her side, untouched,

Stood the brimmed gold; "Bear this," she said, "and pray

He hold a Christian lady apt to learn

A kindly lesson "   But Sir Torel loosed

From off his finger—never loosed before—

The ring she gave him on the parting day;

And ere he drank, behind his veil of beard

Dropped in the cup the ruby, quaffed, and sent.—

Then she, with sad smile, set her lips to drink,

And—something in the Cyprus touching them,

Glanced—gazed—the   ring!—her   ring!—Jove!   how

          she eyes

The wistful eyes of Torel!—how, heartsure,

Under all guise knowing her lord returned,

She springs to meet him coming !—telling all
In one great cry of joy.

              O me ! the rout,
The storm of questions ! stilled, when Torel spake
His name, and, known of all, claimed the Bride Wife,
Maugre the wasted feast, and woful groom.
All hearts but his were light to see Torel;
But Adalieta's lightest, as she plucked
The bridal-veil away.   Something therein—
A lady's dagger—small, and bright, and fine—
Clashed out upon the marble.   "Wherefore that ?"
Asked Torel; answered she, "I knew you true ;
And I could live, so long as I might wait;
But they—they pressed me hard ! my days of grace
Ended to-night—and I had ended too,
Faithful to death, if so thou hadst not come."

THE CALIPH'S DRAUGHT.

———o———

Upon a day in Ramadan—
  When sunset brought an end of fast,
And in his station every man
  Prepared to share the glad repast—
Sate Mohtasim in royal state,
  The pillaw smoked upon the gold;
The fairest slave of those that wait
  Mohtasim's jewelled cup did hold.

Of crystal carven was the cup,
  With turquoise set along the brim,
A lid of amber closed it up;
  'Twas a great king that gave it him.
The slave poured sherbet to the brink,
  Stirred in wild honey and pomegranate,
With snow and rose-leaves cooled the drink,
  And bore it where the Caliph sate.

The Caliph's mouth was dry as bone,

  He swept his beard aside to quaff:—

The news-reader beneath the throne,

  Went droning on with *ghain* and *kaf*.—

The Caliph drew a mighty breath,

  Just then the reader read a word—

And Mohtasim, as grim as death,

  Set down the cup and snatched his sword.

" *Ann' amratan shureefatee !* "

  " Speak clear ! " cries angry Mohtasim ;

" *Fe lasr ind' ilj min ulji,*"—

  Trembling the newsman read to him

How in Ammoria, far from home,

  An Arab girl of noble race

Was captive to a lord of Roum ;

  And how he smote her on the face,

And how she cried, for life afraid,

  "Ya, Mohtasim ! help, O my king ! "

And how the Kafir mocked the maid,

  And laughed, and spake a bitter thing,

" Call louder, fool ! Mohtasim's ears
    Are long as Barak's—if he heed—
Your prophet's ass ; and when he hears,
    He'll come upon a spotted steed !"

The Caliph's face was stern and red,
    He snapped the lid upon the cup ;
" Keep this same sherbet, slave," he said,
    " Till such time as I drink it up.
Wallah ! the stream my drink shall be,
    My hollowed palm my only bowl,
Till I have set that lady free,
    And seen that Roumi dog's head roll."

At dawn the drums of war were beat,
    Proclaiming, " Thus saith Mohtasim,
' Let all my valiant horsemen meet,
    And every soldier bring with him
A spotted steed.'"   So rode they forth,
    A sight of marvel and of fear ;
Pied horses prancing fiercely north ;
    The crystal cup borne in the rear !

When to Ammoria he did win,

    He smote and drove the dogs of Roum,

And rode his spotted stallion in,

    Crying, "*Labbayki!* I am come!"

Then downward from her prison-place

    Joyful the Arab lady crept;

She held her hair before her face,

    She kissed his feet, she laughed and wept.

She pointed where that lord was laid:

    They drew him forth, he whined for grace:

Then with fierce eyes Mohtasim said—

    "She whom thou smotest on the face

Had scorn, because she called her king:

    Lo! he is come! and dost thou think

To live, who didst this bitter thing

    While Mohtasim at peace did drink?"

Flashed the fierce sword—rolled the lord's head;

    The wicked blood smoked in the sand.

"Now bring my cup!" the Caliph said.

    Lightly he took it in his hand,

As down his throat the sweet drink ran
Mohtasim in his saddle laughed,
And cried, " *Taiba asshrab alan !*
By God ! delicious is this draught !"

HINDOO FUNERAL SONG.

———o———

CALL on Rama! call to Rama!
Oh, my brothers, call on Rama!
 For this Dead
 Whom we bring,
Call aloud to mighty Rama.

As we bear him, oh, my brothers,
Call together, very loudly,
 That the Bhûts
 May be scared;
That his spirit pass in comfort.

Turn his feet now, calling "Rama,"
Calling "Rama," who shall take him
 When the flames
 Make an end:
Ram! Ram!—oh, call to Rama.

SONG OF THE SERPENT-CHARMERS.

——o——

COME forth, oh, Snake! come forth, oh, glittering Snake!
Oh shining, lovely, deadly Nâg! appear,
Dance to the music that we make,
   This serpent-song, so sweet and clear,
   Blown on the beaded gourd, so clear,
      So soft and clear.

Oh, dread Lord Snake! come forth and spread thy hood,
And drink the milk and suck the eggs; and show
Thy tongue; and own the tune is good:
   Hear, Maharaj! how hard we blow!
   Ah, Maharaj! for thee we blow;
      See how we blow!

Great Uncle Snake ! creep forth and dance to-day !

This music is the music snakes love best ;

Taste the warm white new milk, and play

    Standing erect, with fangs at rest,

    Dancing on end, sharp fangs at rest,

        Fierce fangs at rest.

Ah, wise Lord Nâg ! thou comest !—Fear thou not !

We make salaam to thee, the Serpent-King,

Draw forth thy folds, knot after knot ;

    Dance, Master ! while we softly sing ;

    Dance, Serpent ! while we play and sing,

        We play and sing.

Dance, dreadful King ! whose kisses strike men dead ;

Dance this side, mighty Snake ! the milk is here !

    [*They seize the Cobra by the neck.*]

Ah, *shabash !* pin his angry head !

    Thou fool ! this nautch shall cost thee dear ;

    Wrench forth his fangs ! this piping clear,

        It costs thee dear !

SONG OF THE FLOUR-MILL.

———o———

TURN the merry mill-stone, Gunga!
  Pour the golden grain in;
Those that twist the Churrak fastest
  The cakes soonest win:
      Good stones, turn!
      The fire begins to burn;
      Gunga, stay not!
      The hearth is nearly hot.
Grind the hard gold to silver,
  Sing quick to the stone;
Feed its mouth with dal and bajri,
  It will feed us anon.

Sing, Gunga! to the mill-stone,
  It helps the wheel hum;

Blithesome hearts and willing elbows
  Make the fine meal come:
    Handsful three
    For you and for me;
    Now it falls white,
    Good stones, bite!
Drive it round and round, my Gunga!
  Sing soft to the stone;
Better corn and churrak-working
  Than idleness and none.

TAZA BA TAZA.

—o—

AKBAR sate high in the ivory hall,
His chief musician he bade them call;
Sing, said the king, that song of glee,
   Taza ba taza, now ba now.
Sing me that music sweet and free,
   Taza ba taza, now ba now;
Here by the fountain sing it thou,
   Taza ba taza, now ba now.

Bending full low, his minstrel took
The Vina down from its painted nook,
Swept the strings of silver so
   Taza ba taza, now ba now;
Made the gladsome Vina go
   Taza ba taza, now ba now;

Sang with light strains and brightsome brow
Taza ba taza, now ba now.

" What is the lay for love most fit ?
What is the melody echoes it ?
Ever in tune and ever meet,
Taza ba taza, now ba now ;
Ever delightful and ever sweet
Taza ba taza, now ba now ;
Soft as the murmur of love's first vow,
Taza ba taza, now ba now."

" What is the bliss that is best on earth ?
Lovers' light whispers and tender mirth ;
Bright gleams the sun on the Green Sea's isle,
But a brighter light has a woman's smile :
Ever, like sunrise, fresh of hue,
Taza ba taza, now ba now ;
Ever, like sunset, splendid and new,
Taza ba taza, now ba now."

" Thereunto groweth the graceful vine
To cool the lips of lovers with wine,

Haste thee and bring the amethyst cup,

That happy lovers may drink it up;

And so renew their gentle play,

  Taza ba taza, now ba now;

Ever delicious and new alway,

  Taza ba taza, now ba now."

" Thereunto sigheth the evening gale

  To freshen the cheeks which love made pale;

  This is why bloometh the scented flower,

  To gladden with grace love's secret bower:

  Love is the zephyr that always blows,

    Taza ba taza, now ba now;

  Love is the rose-bloom that ever glows,

    Taza ba taza, now ba now."

Akbar, the mighty one, smiled to hear

The musical strain so soft and clear;

Danced the diamonds over his brow

  To *taza ba taza, now ba now:*

His lovely ladies rocked in a row

  To *taza ba taza, now ba now;*

Livelier sparkled the fountain's flow,
  Boose sittan ba kaum uzo ;
Swifter and sweeter the strings did go,
  Mutrib i khoosh nuwa bejo ;
Never such singing was heard, I trow ;
  Taza ba taza, now ba now.

THE MUSSULMAN PARADISE.

———o———

(From the Arabic of the Fifty-sixth Súrat of the Korán, entitled " The Inevitable.")

WHEN the Day of Wrath and Mercy cometh, none shall
    doubt it come ;
Unto hell some it shall lower, and exalt to heaven
    some.

When the Earth with great shocks shaketh, and the
    mountains crumble flat,
Quick and Dead shall be divided fourfold :—on this
    side and that.

The " Companions of the Right Hand " (ah ! how joyful
    they will be !)
The " Companions of the Left Hand " (oh ! what misery
    to see !)

Such, moreover, as of old times loved the truth, and
  taught it well,
First in faith, they shall be foremost in reward. The
  rest to hell.

But those souls attaining Allah, oh! the Gardens of
  good cheer
Kept to bless them! Yea, besides the "faithful," many
  shall be there.

Lightly lying on soft couches, beautiful with 'broidered
  gold,
Friends with friends, they shall be served by youths
  immortal, who shall hold

"*Akwâb, abareek*"—cups and goblets, brimming with
  celestial wine,
Wine that hurts not head or stomach : this and fruits
  of heav'n which shine

Bright, desirable ; and rich flesh of what birds they
  relish best.
Yea! and—feasted—there shall soothe them damsels
  fairest, stateliest ;

Damsels, having eyes of wonder, large black eyes, like
  hidden pearls,

"*Lulu-l-maknûn*": Allah grants them for sweet love
  those matchless girls.

Never in that Garden hear they speech of folly, sin, or
  dread,

Only PEACE; "*SALÂMUN*" only; that one word for
  ever said.

PEACE! PEACE! PEACE!—and the "Companions of the
  Right Hand" (ah! those bowers!)

They shall lodge 'mid thornless lote-groves; under
  mawz-trees thick with flowers;

Shaded, fed, by flowing waters; near to fruits that
  never cloy,

Hanging ever ripe for plucking; and at hand the
  tender joy

Of those Maids of Heaven—the Hûris. Lo! to these
  we gave a birth

Specially creating. Lo! they are not as the wives of
  earth.

Ever virginal and stainless, howsooften they embrace,

Always young, and loved, and loving, these are.
    Neither is there grace

Like the grace and bliss the Black-eyed keep for you
    in Paradise;

Oh, "Companions of the Right Hand"! oh! ye others
    who were wise!

DEDICATION OF A POEM FROM THE SANSKRIT.

———o———

SWEET, on the daisies of your English grave
  I lay this little wreath of Indian flowers,
Fragrant for me because the scent they have
  Breathes of the memory of our wedded hours;

For others scentless; and for you, in heaven,
  Too pale and faded, dear dead wife! to wear,
Save that they mean—what makes all fault forgiven—
  That he who brings them lays his heart, too, there.

April 9, 1865.

THE RAJAH'S RIDE.

—o—

A PUNJAB SONG.

Now is the Devil-horse come to Sindh!
 Wah! wah! gooroo!—that is true!
His belly is stuffed with the fire and the wind,
 But a fleeter steed had Runjeet Dehu!

It's forty koss from Lahore to the ford,
 Forty and more to far Jummoo;
Fast may go the Feringhee lord,
 But never so fast as Runjeet Dehu!

Runjeet Dehu was King of the Hill,
 Lord and eagle of every crest;
Now the swords and the spears are still,
 God will have it—and God knows best!

Rajah Runjeet sate in the sky,
   Watching the loaded Kafilas in ;
Affghan, Kashmeree, passing by,
   Paid him pushm to save their skin.

Once he caracoled into the plain,
   Wah! the sparkle of steel on steel !
And up the pass came singing again
   With a lakh of silver borne at his heel.

Once he trusted the Mussulman's word,
   Wah! wah! trust a liar to lie !
Down from his eyrie they tempted my Bird,
   And clipped his wings that he could not fly.

Fettered him fast in far Lahore,
   Fast by the gate at the Runchenee Pûl ;
Sad was the soul of Chunda Kour,
   Glad the merchants of rich Kurnool.

Ten months Runjeet lay in Lahore—
   Wah! a hero's heart is brass !
Ten months never did Chunda Kour
   Braid her hair at the tiring-glass.

There came a steed from Toorkistan,
  Wah! God made him to match the hawk!
Fast beside him the four grooms ran,
  To keep abreast of the Toorkman's walk.

Black as the bear on Iskardoo;
  Savage at heart as a tiger chained;
Fleeter than hawk that ever flew,
  Never a Muslim could ride him reined.

"Runjeet Dehu! come forth from thy hold"—
  Wah! ten months had rusted his chain!
"Ride this Sheitan's liver cold"—
  Runjeet twisted his hand in the mane.

Runjeet sprang to the Toorkman's back,
  Wah! a king on a kingly throne!
Snort, black Sheitan! till nostrils crack,
  Rajah Runjeet sits, a stone.

Three times round the Maidan he rode,
  Touched its neck at the Kashmeree wall,
Struck the spurs till they spirted blood,
  Leapt the rampart before them all!

Breasted the waves of the blue Ravee,
    Forty horsemen mounting behind,
Forty bridle-chains flung free,—
    Wah! wah! better chase the wind!

Chunda Kour sate sad in Jummoo :—
    Hark! what horse-hoof echoes without?
"Rise! and welcome Runjeet Dehu—
    Wash the Toorkman's nostrils out!

"Forty koss he has come, my life!
    Forty koss back he must carry me ;
Rajah Runjeet visits his wife,
    He steals no steed like an Afreedee.

"They bade me teach them how to ride—
    Wah! wah! now I have taught them well!"
Chunda Kour sank low at his side!
    Rajah Runjeet rode the hill.

When he came back to far Lahore—
    Long or ever the night began—
Spake he, "Take your horse once more,
    He carries well—when he bears a man."

Then they gave him a khillut and gold,
    All for his honour and grace and truth;
Sent him back to his mountain-hold—
    Muslim manners have touch of ruth;

Sent him back, with dances and drum—
    Wah! my Rajah Runjeet Dehu!
To Chunda Kour and his Jummoo home—
    Wah! wah! futteh!—wah, gooroo!

TWO BOOKS FROM THE ILIAD
OF INDIA.

TWO BOOKS FROM THE ILIAD OF INDIA.

(Now for the first time translated.)

THERE exist certain colossal, unparalleled, epic poems in the sacred language of India, which were not known to Europe, even by name, till Sir William Jones announced their existence; and which, since his time, have been made public only by fragments—by mere specimens—bearing to those vast treasures of Sanskrit literature such small proportion as cabinet samples of ore have to the riches of a mine. Yet these twain mighty poems contain all the history of ancient India, so far as it can be recovered, together with such inexhaustible details of its political, ·social, and religious life that the antique Hindu world really stands epitomised in them. The Old Testament is not more interwoven with the Jewish race, nor the New Testament with the civilisation of Christendom, nor the Koran with the records and destinies of Islam, than are these two Sanskrit poems — the Mahábhárata and Rámáyana—with that unchanging and teeming population which Her Majesty, Queen Victoria, rules

as Empress of Hindustan. The stories, songs, and
ballads, the histories and genealogies, the nursery
tales and religious discourses, the art, the learning,
the philosophy, the creeds, the moralities, the modes
of thought; the very phrases, sayings, turns of ex-
pression, and daily ideas of the Hindu people, are
taken from these poems. Their children and their
wives are named out of them; so are their cities,
temples, streets, and cattle. They have constituted
the library, the newspaper, and the Bible—generation
after generation—to all the succeeding and countless
millions of Indian people; and it replaces patriotism
with that race and stands in stead of nationality to
possess these two precious and inexhaustible books, and
to drink from them as from mighty and overflowing
rivers. The value ascribed in Hindustan to these yet
little-known epics has transcended all literary standards
established in the West. They are personified, worshipped, and cited from as something divine. To read
or even listen to them is thought by the devout Hindu
sufficiently meritorious to bring prosperity to his household here and happiness in the next world; they are
held also to give wealth to the poor, health to the sick,
wisdom to the ignorant; and the recitation of certain
parvas and *shlokas* in them can fill the household of
the barren, it is believed, with children. A concluding
passage of the great poem says:—

"The reading of this Mahábhárata destroys all sin and pro-
duces virtue; so much so, that the pronunciation of a single

shloka is sufficient to wipe away much guilt. This Mahá-bhárata contains the history of the gods, of the Rishis in heaven and those on earth, of the Gandharvas and the Rák-shasas. It also contains the life and actions of the one God, holy, immutable, and true,—who is Krishna, who is the creator and the ruler of this universe; who is seeking the welfare of his creation by means of his incomparable and indestructible power; whose actions are celebrated by all sages; who has bound human beings in a chain, of which one end is life and the other death; on whom the Rishis meditate, and a know-ledge of whom imparts unalloyed happiness to their hearts, and for whose gratification and favour all the daily devotions are performed by all worshippers. If a man reads the Mahá-bhárata and has faith in its doctrines, he is free from all sin, and ascends to heaven after his death."

In order to explain the portion of this Indian epic, here for the first time published in English verse, I reprint a brief summary of its plot:—

The "great war of Bharat" has its first scenes in Hastinapur, an ancient and vanished city, formerly situated about sixty miles north-east of the modern Delhi. The Ganges has washed away even the ruins of this the metropolis of King Bharat's dominions. The poem opens with a "sacrifice of snakes;" but this is a prelude, connected merely by a curious legend with the real beginning. That beginning is reached when the five sons of "King Pandu the Pale" and the five sons of "King Dhritarashtra the Blind," both of them descendants of Bharat, are being brought up together in the palace. The first were called Pandavas, the last Kauravas, and their lifelong feud is the main subject of the epic. Yudhishthira, Bhíma, Arjuna, Nakula, and Sahadeva are the Pandava princes. Duryodhana

L

is chief of the Kauravas.   They are instructed by one
master, Drona, a Brahman, in the arts of war and
peace, and learn to manage and brand cattle, hunt wild
animals, and tame horses.   There is in the early portion
a striking picture of an Aryan tournament, wherein the
young cousins display their skill, "highly arrayed, amid
vast crowds," and Arjuna especially distinguishes himself.   Clad in golden mail, he shows amazing feats with
sword and bow.   He shoots twenty-one arrows into the
hollow of a buffalo-horn while his chariot whirls along;
he throws the "chakra," or sharp quoit, without once
missing his victim; and, after winning the prizes,
kneels respectfully at the feet of his instructor to
receive his crown.   The cousins, after this, march out
to fight with a neighbouring king, and the Pandavas,
who are always the favoured family in the poem, win
most of the credit, so that Yudhishthira is elected from
among them *Yuvaraj*, or heir apparent.   This incenses
Duryodhana, who, by appealing to his father, Dhritarashtra, procures a division of the kingdom, the Pandavas
being sent to Vacanavat, now Allahabad.   All this part
of the story refers obviously to the advances gradually
made by the Aryan conquerors of India into the jungles
peopled by aborigines.   Forced to quit their new city,
the Pandavas hear of the marvellous beauty of Draupadí,
whose *Swayamvara*, or "choice of a suitor," is about to
be celebrated at Kâmpilya.   This again furnishes a
strange and glittering picture of the old times; vast
masses of holiday people, with rajahs, elephants, troops,

jugglers, dancing-women, and showmen, are gathered
in a gay encampment round the pavilion of the King
Draupada, whose lovely daughter is to take for her
husband (on the well-understood condition that she
approves of him) the fortunate archer who can strike
the eye of a golden fish, whirling round upon the top
of a tall pole, with an arrow shot from an enormously
strong bow. The princess, adorned with radiant gems,
holds a garland of flowers in her hand for the victorious
suitor; but none of the rajahs can bend the bow.
Arjuna, disguised as a Brahman, performs the feat with
ease, and his youth and grace win the heart of Draupadí
more completely than his skill. The princess henceforth follows the fortunes of the brothers, and, by a
strange ancient custom, lives with them in common.
The Pandavas, now allied to the King Draupada and
become strong, are so much dreaded by the Kauravas
that they are invited back again, for safety's sake, to
Hastinapura, and settle near it in the city of Indraprastha, now Delhi. The reign of Yudhishthira and
his brothers is very prosperous there; "every subject
was pious; there were no liars, thieves, or cheats; no
droughts, floods, or locusts; no conflagrations nor in-
vaders, nor parrots to eat up the grain."

The Pandava king, having subdued all enemies, now
performs the *Rajasuya,* or ceremony of supremacy,—
and here again occur wonderfully interesting pictures.
Duryodhana comes thither, and his jealousy is inflamed
by the magnificence of the rite. Among other curious

incidents is one which seems to show that glass was already known. A pavilion is paved with "black crystal," which the Kaurava prince mistakes for water, and "draws up his garments lest he should be wetted." But now approaches a turning-point in the epic. Furious at the wealth and fortune of his cousins, Duryodhana invites them to Hastinapura to join in a great gambling festival. The passion for play was as strong apparently with these antique Hindus as that for fighting or for love: "No true Kshatriya must ever decline a challenge to combat or to dice." The brothers go to the entertainment, which is to ruin their prosperity; for Sakuni, the most skilful and lucky gambler, has loaded the "coupun," so as to win every throw. Mr. Wheeler's excellent summary again says:—

"Then Yudhishthira and Sakuni sat down to play, and whatever Yudhishthira laid as stakes Duryodhana laid something of equal value ; but Yudhishthira lost every game. He first lost a very beautiful pearl ; next a thousand bags each containing a thousand pieces of gold ; next a great piece of gold so pure that it was as soft as wax ; next a chariot set with jewels and hung all round with golden bells ; next a thousand war-elephants with golden howdahs set with diamonds ; next a lakh of slaves all dressed in rich garments ; next a lakh of beautiful slave-girls, adorned from head to foot with golden ornaments ; next all the remainder of his goods ; next all his cattle ; and then the whole of his Ráj, excepting only the lands which had been granted to the Brahmans."

After this tremendous run of ill-luck, he madly stakes Draupadí the Beautiful, and loses her. The princess is dragged away by the hair, and Duryodhana mockingly bids her come and sit upon his knee, for which Bhíma the Pandava swears that he will some day break his thigh-bone,—a vow which is duly kept. But the blind old king rebukes this fierce elation of the winner, restores Draupadí, and declares that they must throw another main to decide who shall leave Hastinapura. The cheating Sakuni cogs the dice again, and the Pandavas must now go away into the forest, and let no man know them by name for thirteen years. They depart, Draupadí unbinding her long black hair, and vowing never to fasten it back again till the hands of Bhíma, the strong man among the Pandavas, are red with the punishment of the Kauravas. "Then he shall tie my tresses up again, when his fingers are dripping with Duhsasana's blood."

There follow long episodes of their adventures in the jungle till the time when the Pandavas emerge, and, still disguised, take up their residence in King Viráta's city. Here the vicissitudes of Draupadí as a handmaid of the queen, of Bhíma as the palace wrestler, of Arjuna disguised as a eunuch, and of Nakula, Sahadeva, and Yudhishthira, acting as herdsmen and attendants, are most absorbing and dramatic. The virtue of Draupadí, assailed by a prince of the State, is terribly defended by the giant Bhíma ; and when the Kauravas, suspecting the presence in the place of their cousins, attack Viráta, Arjuna drives the chariot of the heir apparent, and victoriously repulses them with his awful bow Gandiva.

After all these evidences of prowess and the help

afforded in the battle, the King of Viráta discovers the
princely rank of the Pandavas, and gives his daughter
in marriage to the son of Arjuna. A great council is
then held to consider the question of declaring war on
the Kauravas, at which the speeches are quite Homeric,
the god Krishna taking part. The decision is to
prepare for war, but to send an embassy first. Meantime Duryodhana and Arjuna engage in a singular
contest to obtain the aid of Krishna, whom both of
them seek out. This celestial hero is asleep when they
arrive, and the proud Kaurava, as Lord of Indraprastha,
sits down at his head; Arjuna, more reverently, takes
a place at his feet. Krishna, awaking, offers to give
his vast army to one of them, and himself as counsellor
to the other; and Arjuna gladly allows Duryodhana
to take the army, which turns out much the worse
bargain. The embassy, meantime, is badly received;
but it is determined to reply by a counter-message,
while warlike preparations continue. There is a great
deal of useless negotiation, against which Draupadí
protests, like another Constance, saying, "War, war!
no peace! Peace is to me a war!" Krishna consoles
her with the words, "Weep not! the time has nearly
come when the Kauravas will be slain, both great and
small, and their wives will mourn as you have been
mourning." The ferocity of the chief of the Kauravas
prevails over the wise counsels of the blind old king
and the warnings of Krishna, so that the fatal conflict
must now begin upon the plain of Kurukshetra.

All is henceforth martial and stormy in the "parvas" that ensue. The two enormous hosts march to the field, generalissimos are selected, and defiances of the most violent and abusive sort exchanged. Yet there are traces of a singular civilisation in the rules which the leaders draw up to be observed in the war. Thus, no stratagems are to be used; the fighting men are to fraternise, if they will, after each combat; none may slay the flier, the unarmed, the charioteer, or the beater of the drum; horsemen are not to attack footmen, and nobody is to fling a spear till the preliminary challenges are finished; nor may any third man interfere when two combatants are engaged. These curious regulations —which would certainly much embarrass Von Moltke —are, sooth to say, not very strictly observed, and, no doubt, were inserted at a later age in the body of the poem by its Brahman editors. Those same interpolaters have overloaded the account of the eighteen days of terrific battle which follow with many episodes and interruptions, some very eloquent and philosophic; indeed, the whole *Bhagavad-Gîta* comes in hereabouts as a religious interlude. Essays on laws, morals, and the sciences are grafted, with lavish indifference to the continuous flow of the narrative, upon its most important portions; but there is enough of solid and tremendous fighting, notwithstanding, to pale the crimson pages of the Greek Iliad itself. The field glitters, indeed, with kings and princes in panoply of gold and jewels, who engage in mighty and varied combats, till the earth swims in blood, and the heavens themselves are obscured with dust and flying weapons. One by one the Kaurava chiefs are slain, and Bhíma, the giant, at last meets in arms Duhsasana, the Kaurava prince who had dragged Draupadí by the hair. He strikes him down with the terrible mace of iron, after which he cuts off his head, and drinks of his blood, saying, "Never have I tasted a draught so delicious as this." So furious now becomes the war that even the just and mild Arjuna commits two breaches of Aryan chivalry, —killing an enemy while engaged with a third man, and shooting Karna dead while he is extricating his chariot-wheel and without a weapon. At last none are left of the chief Kauravas except Duryodhana, who retires from the field and hides in an island of the lake. The Pandavas find him out, and heap such reproaches on him that the surly warrior comes forth at length, and agrees to fight with Bhíma. The duel proves of a tremendous nature, and is decided by an act of treachery; for Arjuna, standing by, reminds Bhíma, by a gesture, of his oath to break the thigh of Duryodhana, because he had bidden Draupadí sit on his knee. The giant takes the hint, and strikes a foul blow, which cripples the Kaurava hero, and he falls helpless to earth. After this the Pandava princes are declared victorious, and Yudhishthira is proclaimed king.

The great poem soon softens its martial music into a pathetic strain. The dead have to be burned, and the living reconciled to their new lords; while after-

wards King Yudhishthira is installed in high state
with "chámaras, golden umbrellas, elephants, and singing." He is enthroned facing towards the east, and
touches rice, flowers, earth, gold, silver, and jewels,
in token of owning all the products of his realm.
Being thus firmly seated on his throne, with his cousins
round him, the Rajah prepares to celebrate the most
magnificent of ancient Hindu rites,—the *Aswamedha*,
or Sacrifice of the Horse. It is difficult to raise the
thoughts of a modern and Western public to the
solemnity, majesty, and marvel of this antique Oriental
rite, as viewed by Hindus. The monarch who was
powerful enough to perform it chose a horse of pure
white colour, "like the moon," with a saffron tail, and
a black right ear; or the animal might be all black,
without a speck of colour. This steed, wearing a gold
plate on its forehead, with the royal name inscribed,
was turned loose, and during a whole year the king's
army was bound to follow its wanderings. Whitherso-
ever it went, the ruler of the invaded territory must
either pay homage to the king, and join him with his
warriors, or accept battle; but whether conquered or
peacefully submitting, all these princes must follow
the horse, and at the end of the year assist at the
sacrifice of the consecrated animal. Moreover, during
the whole year the king must restrain all passion, live
a perfectly purified life, and sleep on the bare ground.
The white horse could not be loosened until the night
of the full moon in *Chaitra*, which answers to the

latter half of March and the first half of April,—in fact, at Easter-time; and it may be observed here that this is not the only strange coincidence in the sacrifice. It was thus an adventure of romantic conquest, mingled with deep religion and arrogant ostentation; and the entire description of the *Aswamedha* would prove most interesting. The horse is found, is adorned with the golden plate, and turned loose, wandering into distant regions; where the army of Arjuna—for it was he who led Yudhishthira's forces—goes through twelve amazing adventures. They come, for instance, to a land of Amazons, all of wonderful beauty, wearing armour of pearls and gold, and equally fatal either to love or to fight with. These dazzling enemies, however, finally submit, as also the Rajah of the rich city of Babhru-váhan, which possessed high walls of solid silver, and was lighted with precious jewels for lamps. The serpent people, in the same way, who live beneath the earth in the city of Vasuki, yield, after combat, to Arjuna. A thousand million semi-human snakemen dwelt there, with wives of consummate loveliness, possessing in their realm gems which would restore dead people to life, as well as a fountain of perpetual youth. Finally, Arjuna's host marches back in great glory, and with a vast train of vanquished monarchs, to the city of Hastinapura, where all the subject kings have audience of Yudhishthira, and the immense preparations begin for the sacrifice of the snow-white horse.

After all these stately celebrations, it might be

expected that the great poem would conclude with the
established glories of the ancient dynasty. But if the
martial part of the colossal epic is "Kshatriyan," and
the religious episodes "Brahmanic," the conclusion
breathes the spirit of Buddhism. Yudhishthira sits
grandly on the throne; but earthly greatness does not
content the soul of man, nor can riches render weary
hearts happy. A wonderful scene, which reads like a
rebuke from the dead addressed to the living upon the
madness of all war, occurs in this part of the poem.
The Pandavas and the old King Dhritarashtra being
together by the banks of the Ganges, the great saint
Vyása undertakes to bring back to them all the
departed, slain in their fratricidal conflict. The spec-
tacle is at once terrible and tender.

But this revealing of the invisible world deepens the
discontent of the princes, and when the sage Vyása
tells them that their prosperity is near its end, they
determine to leave their kingdom to younger princes,
and to set out with their faces towards Mount Meru,
where is Indra's heaven. If, haply, they may reach it,
there will be an end of this world's joys and sorrows,
and "union with the Infinite" will be obtained. My
translations from the Sanskrit of the two concluding
parvas of the poem (of which the above is a swift summary) describe the "Last Journey" of the princes and
their "Entry into Heaven;" and herein occurs one of
the noblest religious apologues not only of this great
Epic but of any creed,—a beautiful fable of faithful

love which may be contrasted, to the advantage of the
Hindu teaching, with any Scriptural representations
of Death, and of Love, " which stronger is than Death."
There is always something selfish in the anxiety of
Orthodox people to save their own souls, and our best
religious language is not free from that taint of pious
egotism.   The Parvas of the Mahábhárata which contain Yudhishthira's approach to Indra's paradise teach,
on the contrary, that deeper and better lesson nobly
enjoined by an American poet—

> " The gate of heaven opens to none alone,
>   Save thou one soul, and it shall save thine own."

These prefatory remarks seemed necessary to intro-
duce the subjoined close paraphrase of the " Book of
the Great Journey,"—and the " Book of the Entry into
Heaven ; " being the Seventeenth and Eighteenth
Parvas of the noble but, as yet, almost unknown
Mahábhárata.

THE MAHAPRASTHÁNIKA PARVA OF THE MAHÁBHÁRATA.

" THE GREAT JOURNEY."

To Narayen, Lord of lords, be glory given,

To sweet Saraswati, the Queen in Heaven,

To great Vyása, eke, pay reverence due,

So shall this story its high course pursue.

Then Janmejaya prayed: "Thou Singer, say,
What wrought the princes of the Pandavas
On tidings of the battle so ensued,
And Krishna, gone on high?"

Answered the Sage:
" On tidings of the wreck of Vrishni's race,
King Yudhishthira of the Pandavas
Was minded to be done with earthly things,
And to Arjuna spake: 'O noble Prince,
Time endeth all; we linger, noose on neck,
Till the last day tightens the line, and kills.
Let us go forth to die, being yet alive.'
And Kunti's son, the great Arjuna, said:
'Let us go forth to die!—Time slayeth all;
We will find Death, who seeketh other men.'
And Bhimasena, hearing, answered: 'Yea!
We will find Death!' and Sahadev cried: 'Yea!'
And his twin brother Nakula: whereat
The princes set their faces for the Mount.

" But Yudhishthira— ere he left his realm,
To seek high ending—summoned Yuyutsu,

Surnamed of fights, and set him over all,

Regent, to rule in Parikshita's name

Nearest the throne ; and Parikshita king

He crowned, and unto old Subhadra said :

‘ This, thy son's son, shall wear the Kuru crown,

And Yadu's offspring, Vajra, shall be first

In Yadu's house.   Bring up the little prince

Here in our Hastinpur, but Vajra keep

At Indraprasth ; and let it be thy last

Of virtuous works to guard the lads, and guide.’

“ So ordering ere he went, the righteous king

Made offering of white water, heedfully,

To Vasudev, to Rama, and the rest,—

All funeral rites performing ; next he spread

A funeral feast, whereat there sate as guests

Narada, Dwaipayana, Bharadwaj,

And Markandeya, rich in saintly years,

And Tajnavalkya, Hari, and the priests.

Those holy ones he fed with dainty meats

In kingliest wise, naming the name of Him

Who bears the bow : and—that it should be well

For him and his—gave to the Brahmanas

Jewels of gold and silver, lakhs on lakhs,
Fair broidered cloths, gardens and villages,
Chariots and steeds and slaves.

                  " Which being done,—
O Best of Bhârat's line !—he bowed him low
Before his Guru's feet,—at Kripa's feet,
That sage all honoured,—saying, ' Take my prince ;
Teach Parikshita as thou taughtest me ;
For hearken, ministers and men of war !
Fixed is my mind to quit all earthly state.'
Full sore of heart were they, and sore the folk
To hear such speech, and bitter spread the word
Through town and country, that the king would go ;
And all the people cried, ' Stay with us, Lord ! '
But Yudhishthira knew the time was come,
Knew that life passes and that virtue lasts,
And put aside their love.

                  " So—with farewells
Tenderly took of lieges and of lords—
Girt he for travel, with his princely kin,

Great Yudhishthira, Dharma's royal son.

Crest-gem and belt and ornaments he stripped

From off his body, and for broidered robe

A rough dress donned, woven of jungle-bark;

And what he did—O Lord of men!—so did

Arjuna, Bhíma, and the twin-born pair,

Nakula with Sahadev, and she—in grace

The peerless—Draupadí.   Lastly these six,

Thou son of Bhârata! in solemn form

Made the high sacrifice of Naishtiki,

Quenching their flames in water at the close;

And so set forth, 'midst wailing of all folk

And tears of women, weeping most to see

The Princess Draupadí—that lovely prize

Of the great gaming, Draupadí the Bright—

Journeying afoot; but she and all the Five

Rejoiced, because their way lay heavenwards.

" Seven were they, setting forth,—princess and king.

The king's four brothers, and a faithful dog.

Those left Hastinapur; but many a man,

And all the palace household, followed them

The first sad stage; and, ofttimes prayed to part,

Put parting off for love and pity, still
Sighing ' A little farther ! '—till day waned ;
Then one by one they turned, and Kripa said,
' Let all turn back, Yuyutsu !   These must go.'
So came they homewards, but the Snake-King's child,
Ulùpi, leapt in Ganges, losing them ;
And Chitranâgad with her people went
Mournful to Munipoor, whilst the three queens
Brought Parikshita in.

            " Thus wended they,
Pandu's five sons and loveliest Draupadí,
Tasting no meat, and journeying due east ;
On righteousness their high hearts bent, to heaven
Their souls assigned ; and steadfast trode their feet,
By faith upborne, past nullah, ran, and wood,
River and jheel and plain.   King Yudhishthir
Walked foremost, Bhíma followed, after him
Arjuna, and the twin-born brethren next,
Nakula with Sahadev ; in whose still steps—
O Best of Bhârat's offspring !—Draupadí,
That gem of women, paced ; with soft, dark face,—
Beautiful, wonderful !—and lustrous eyes,

M

Clear-lined like lotus-petals; last the dog,
Following the Pandavas.

               " At length they reach
The far Lauchityan Sea, which foameth white
Under Udayachâla's ridge.—Know ye
That all this while Nakula had not ceased
Bearing the holy bow, named Gandiva,
And jewelled quiver, ever filled with shafts
Though one should shoot a thousand thousand times.
Here—broad across their path—the heroes see
Agni, the god.   As though a mighty hill
Took form of front and breast and limb, he spake.
Seven streams of shining splendour rayed his brow,
While the dread voice said : ' I am Agni, chiefs !
O sons of Pandu, I am Agni !   Hail !
O long-armed Yudhishthira, blameless king,—
O warlike Bhíma,—O Arjuna, wise,—
O brothers twin-born from a womb divine,—
Hear ! I am Agni, who consumed the wood
By will of Narayan for Arjuna's sake.
Let this your brother give Gandiva back,—
The matchless bow : the use for it is o'er.

That gem-ringed battle-discus which he whirled

Cometh again to Krishna in his hand

For avatars to be; and need is none

Henceforth of this most excellent bright bow,

Gandiva, which I brought for Partha's aid

From high Varuna.   Let it be returned.

Cast it herein!'

        " And all the princes said,

'Cast it, dear brother!'   So Arjuna threw

Into that sea the quiver ever-filled,

And glittering bow.   Then led by Agni's light,

Unto the south they turned, and so south-west,

And afterwards right west, until they saw

Dwaraka, washed and bounded by a main

Loud-thundering on its shores; and here—O Best!—

Vanished the God; while yet those heroes walked,

Now to the north-west bending, where long coasts

Shut in the sea of salt, now to the north,

Accomplishing all quarters, journeyed they;

The earth their altar of high sacrifice,

Which these most patient feet did pace around

Till Meru rose.

"At last it rose!   These Six,
Their senses subjugate, their spirits pure,
Wending alone, came into sight—far off
In the eastern sky—of awful Himavan;
And, midway in the peaks of Himavan,
Meru, the Mountain of all mountains, rose,
Whose head is Heaven; and under Himavan
Glared a wide waste of sand, dreadful as death.

" Then, as they hastened o'er the deadly waste,
Aiming for Meru, having thoughts at soul
Infinite, eager,—lo! Draupadí reeled,
With faltering heart and feet; and Bhíma turned
Gazing upon her; and that hero spake
To Yudhishthira: 'Master, Brother, King
Why doth she fail?   For never all her life
Wrought our sweet lady one thing wrong, I think.
Thou knowest, make us know, why hath she failed?'

' Then Yudhishthira answered: ' Yea, one thing.
She loved our brother better than all else,—
Better than heaven: that was her tender sin,
Fault of a faultless soul; she pays for that.'

" So spake the monarch, turning not his eyes,
  Though Draupadí lay dead—striding straight on
  For Meru, heart-full of the things of heaven,
  Perfect and firm. But yet a little space,
  And Sahadev fell down, which Bhíma seeing,
  Cried once again : ' O King, great Madri's son
  Stumbles and sinks. Why hath he sunk ?—so true,
  So brave and steadfast, and so free from pride ! '

" ' He was not free,' with countenance still fixed,
  Quoth Yudhishthira ; ' he was true and fast
  And wise, yet wisdom made him proud ; he hid
  One little hurt of soul, but now it kills.'

" So saying, he strode on—Kunti's strong son—
  And Bhíma, and Arjuna followed him,
  And Nakula, and the hound ; leaving behind
  Sahadev in the sands. But Nakula,
  Weakened and grieved to see Sahadev fall—
  His loved twin-brother—lagged and stayed ; and next
  Prone on his face he fell, that noble face
  Which had no match for beauty in the land,—
  Glorious and godlike Nakula ! Then sighed

Bhíma anew: 'Brother and Lord ! the man
Who never erred from virtue, never broke
Our fellowship, and never in the world
Was matched for goodly perfectness of form
Or gracious feature,—Nakula has fallen !'

" But Yudhishthira, holding fixed his eyes,—
That changeless, faithful, all-wise king,—replied :
'Yea, but he erred.   The godlike form he wore
Beguiled him to believe none like to him,
And he alone desirable, and things
Unlovely to be slighted.   Self-love slays
Our noble brother.   Bhíma, follow !   Each
Pays what his debt was.'

                    " Which Arjuna heard,
Weeping to see them fall ; and that stout son
Of Pandu, that destroyer of his foes,
That prince, who drove through crimson waves of war,
In old days, with his chariot-steeds of milk,
He, the arch-hero, sank !   Beholding this,—
The yielding of that soul unconquerable,
Fearless, divine, from Sakra's self derived,

Arjuna's,—Bhíma cried aloud: ' O king!
This man was surely perfect.   Never once,
Not even in slumber when the lips are loosed,
Spake he one word that was not true as truth.
Ah, heart of gold, why art thou broke?   O King!
Whence falleth he?'

      " And Yudhishthira said,
Not pausing: ' Once he lied, a lordly lie!
He bragged—our brother—that a single day
Should see him utterly consume, alone,
All those his enemies,—which could not be.
Yet from a great heart sprang the unmeasured speech.
Howbeit, a finished hero should not shame
Himself in such wise, nor his enemy,
If he will faultless fight and blameless die:
This was Arjuna's sin.   Follow thou me!'

" So the king still went on.   But Bhíma next
  Fainted, and stayed upon the way, and sank;
  Yet, sinking cried, behind the steadfast prince:
  ' Ah, brother, see! I die!   Look upon me,

Thy well-belovèd!   Wherefore falter I,
Who strove to stand?'

            "And Yudhishthira said:
'More than was well the goodly things of earth
Pleased thee, my pleasant brother! Light the offence,
And large thy virtue; but the o'er-fed flesh
Plumed itself over spirit.   Pritha's son,
For this thou failest, who so near didst gain.'

"Thenceforth alone the long-armed monarch strode,
  Not looking back,—nay! not for Bhíma's sake,—
  But walking with his face set for the Mount:
  And the hound followed him,—only the hound.

"After the deathly sands, the Mount! and lo!
  Sakra shone forth,—the God, filling the earth
  And heavens with thunder of his chariot-wheels.
  'Ascend,' he said, 'with me, Pritha's great son!'
  But Yudhishthira answered, sore at heart
  For those his kinsfolk, fallen on the way:
  'O Thousand-eyed, O Lord of all the Gods,
  Give that my brothers come with me, who fell!

Not without them is Swarga sweet to me.

She too, the dear and kind and queenly,—she

Whose perfect virtue Paradise must crown,—

Grant her to come with us! Dost thou grant this?'

" The God replied: 'In heaven thou shalt see

Thy kinsmen and the queen—these will attain—

With Krishna.   Grieve no longer for thy dead,

Thou chief of men! their mortal covering stripped,

They have their places; but to thee the gods

Allot an unknown grace: thou shalt go up

Living and in thy form to the immortal homes.'

" But the king answered: ' O thou Wisest One,

Who know'st what was, and is, and is to be,

Still one more grace! This hound hath ate with me,

Followed me, loved me: must I leave him now?'

" 'Monarch,' spake Indra, 'thou art now as We,—

Deathless, divine; thou art become a god;

Glory and power and gifts celestial,

And all the joys of heaven are thine for aye:

What hath a beast with these? Leave here thy hound.'

"Yet Yudhishthira answered: 'O Most High,
    O Thousand-eyed and Wisest! can it be
    That one exalted should seem pitiless?
    Nay, let me lose such glory: for its sake
    I would not leave one living thing I loved.'

"Then sternly Indra spake: 'He is unclean,
    And into Swarga such shall enter not.
    The Krodhavasha's hand destroys the fruits
    Of sacrifice, if dogs defile the fire.
    Bethink thee, Dharmaraj, quit now this beast!
    That which is seemly is not hard of heart.'

"Still he replied: ''Tis written that to spurn
    A suppliant equals in offence to slay
    A twice-born; wherefore, not for Swarga's bliss
    Quit I, Mahendra, this poor clinging dog,—
    So without any hope or friend save me,
    So wistful, fawning for my faithfulness,
    So agonized to die, unless I help
    Who among men was called steadfast and just.'

" Quoth Indra: ' Nay! the altar-flame is foul

  Where a dog passeth; angry angels sweep

  The ascending smoke aside, and all the fruits

  Of offering, and the merit of the prayer

  Of him whom a hound toucheth. Leave it here !

  He that will enter heaven must enter pure.

  Why didst thou quit thy brethren on the way,

  Quit Krishna, quit the dear-loved Draupadí,

  Attaining, firm and glorious, to this Mount

  Through perfect deeds, to linger for a brute ?

  Hath Yudhishthira vanquished self, to melt

  With one poor passion at the door of bliss ?

  Stay'st thou for this, who didst not stay for them,—

  Draupadí, Bhíma ? '

                 " But the king yet spake:

' 'Tis known that none can hurt or help the dead.

  They, the delightful ones, who sank and died,

  Following my footsteps, could not live again

  Though I had turned,—therefore I did not turn ;

  But could help profit, I had turned to help.

  There be four sins, O Sakra, grievous sins:

  The first is making suppliants despair,

The second is to slay a nursing wife,

The third is spoiling Brahmans' goods by force,

The fourth is injuring an ancient friend.

These four I deem not direr than the sin,

If one, in coming forth from woe to weal,

Abandon any meanest comrade then.'

" Straight as he spake, brightly great Indra smiled ;

Vanished the hound ;—and in its stead stood there

The Lord of Death and Justice, Dharma's self !

Sweet were the words which fell from those dread lips,

Precious the lovely praise : ' O thou true king,

Thou that dost bring to harvest the good seed

Of Pandu's righteousness ; thou that hast ruth

As he before, on all which lives !—O Son,

I tried thee in the Dwaita wood, what time

The Yaksha smote them, bringing water ; then

Thou prayedst for Nakula's life—tender and just—

Not Bhíma's nor Arjuna's, true to both,

To Madrî as to Kuntî, to both queens.

Hear thou my word ! Because thou didst not mount

This car divine, lest the poor hound be shent

Who looked to thee, lo ! there is none in heaven

Shall sit above thee, King!—Bhârata's son,

Enter thou now to the eternal joys,

Living and in thy form. Justice and Love

Welcome thee, Monarch! thou shalt throne with
  us!'

" Thereat those mightiest Gods, in glorious train,

Mahendra, Dharma,—with bright retinue

Of Maruts, Saints, Aswin-Kumāras, Nats,

Spirits and Angels,—bore the king aloft,

The thundering chariot first, and after it

Those airy-moving Presences. Serene,

Clad in great glory, potent, wonderful,

They glide at will,—at will they know and see,

At wish their wills are wrought; for these are pure,

Passionless, hallowed, perfect, free of earth.

In such celestial midst the Pandu king

Soared upward; and a sweet light filled the sky

And fell on earth, cast by his face and form,

Transfigured as he rose; and there was heard

The voice of Narad,—it is he who sings,

Sitting in heaven, the deeds that good men do

In all the quarters,—Narad, chief of bards,

Narad the wise, who laudeth purity,—
So cried he: 'Thou art risen, unmatchèd king,
Whose greatness is above all royal saints.
Hail, son of Pandu! like to thee is none
Now or before among the sons of men,
Whose fame hath filled the three wide worlds, who
    com'st
Bearing thy mortal body, which doth shine
With radiance as a god's.'

             "The glad king heard
Narad's loud praise; he saw the immortal gods,—
Dharma, Mahendra; and dead chiefs and saints,
Known upon earth, in blessèd heaven he saw;
But only those. 'I do desire,' he said,
'That region, be it of the Blest as this,
Or of the Sorrowful some otherwhere,
Where my dear brothers are, and Draupadí.
I cannot stay elsewhere! I see them not!'

"Then answer made Purandará, the God:
'O thou compassionate and noblest One,
Rest in the pleasures which thy deeds have gained.

How, being as are the Gods, canst thou live bound

By mortal chains?   Thou art become of Us,

Who live above hatred and love, in bliss

Pinnacled, safe, supreme.   Sun of thy race,

Thy brothers cannot reach where thou hast climbed!

Most glorious lord of men, let not thy peace

Be touched by stir of earth!   Look! this is Heaven.

See where the saints sit, and the happy souls,

Siddhas and angels, and the gods who live

For ever and for ever.'

                        "' King of gods,'

Spake Yudhishthira, 'but I will not live

A little space without those souls I loved.

O Slayer of the demons! let me go

Where Bhíma and my brothers are, and she,

My Draupadí, the princess with the face

Softer and darker than the Vrihat-leaf,

And soul as sweet as are its odours.   Lo!

Where they have gone, there will I surely go.' "

THE ILIAD OF INDIA.

—o—

THE SWARGAROHANA PARVA OF THE MAHÁBHÁRATA; OR, "THE ENTRY INTO HEAVEN."

To Narayen, Lord of lords, be glory given,
To Queen Saraswati be praise in heaven;
Unto Vyâsa pay the reverence due,—
So may this story its high course pursue.

THEN Janmejaya said : " I am fain to learn
How it befell with my great forefathers,
The Pandu chiefs and Dhritarashtra's sons,
Being to heaven ascended.   If thou know'st,—
And thou know'st all, whom wise Vyâsa taught,—
Tell me, how fared it with those mighty souls ? "

Answered the Sage : " Hear of thy forefathers—
Great Yudhishthira and the Pandu lords—

How it befell. When thus the blameless king

Was entered into heaven, there he beheld

Duryodhana, his foe, throned as a god

Amid the gods; splendidly sate that prince,

Peaceful and proud, the radiance of his brows

Far-shining like the sun's ; and round him thronged

Spirits of light, with Sádhyas,—companies

Goodly to see. But when the king beheld

Duryodhana in bliss, and not his own,—

Not Draupadí, nor Bhíma, nor the rest,—

With quick-averted face and angry eyes

The monarch spake: ' Keep heaven for such as these

If these come here!   I do not wish to dwell

Where he is, whom I hated rightfully,

Being a covetous and witless prince,

Whose deed it was that in wild fields of war

Brothers and friends by mutual slaughter fell,

While our swords smote, sharpened so wrathfully

By all those wrongs borne wandering in the woods :

But Draupadí's the deepest wrong, for he—

He who sits there—haled her before the court,

Seizing that sweet and virtuous lady—he !—

With grievous hand wound in her tresses. Gods,

N

I cannot look upon him! Sith 'tis so,

Where are my brothers? Thither will I go!'

"Smiling, bright Narada, the Sage, replied:

'Speak thou not rashly! Say not this, O King!

Those who come here lay enmities aside.

O Yudhishthira, long-armed monarch, hear!

Duryodhana is cleansed of sin; he sits

Worshipful as the saints, worshipped by saints

And kings who lived and died in virtue's path,

Attaining to the joys which heroes gain

Who yield their breath in battle. Even so

He that did wrong thee, knowing not thy worth,

Hath won before thee hither, raised to bliss

For lordliness, and valour free of fear.

Ah, well-belovèd Prince! ponder thou not

The memory of that gaming, nor the griefs

Of Draupadí, nor any vanished hurt

Wrought in the passing shows of life by craft

Or wasteful war. Throne happy at the side

Of this thy happy foeman,—wiser now;

For here is Paradise, thou chief of men!

And in its holy air hatreds are dead.'

" Thus by such lips addressed the Pandu king
   Answered uncomforted : ' Duryodhana,
   If he attains, attains; yet not the less
   Evil he lived and ill he died,—a heart
   Impious and harmful, bringing woes to all,
   To friends and foes. His was the crime which cost
   Our land its warriors, horses, elephants ;
   His the black sin that set us in the field,
   Burning for rightful vengeance. Ye are gods,
   And just; and ye have granted heaven to him.
   Show me the regions, therefore, where they dwell,
   My brothers, those, the noble-souled, the loyal,
   Who kept the sacred laws, who swerved no step
   From virtue's path, who spake the truth, and lived
   Foremost of warriors. Where is Kunti's son,
   The hero-hearted Karna ? Where are gone
   Sátyaki, Dhrishtadyumna, with their sons ?
   And where those famous chiefs who fought for me,
   Dying a splendid death ? I see them not.
   O Narada, I see them not ! No King
   Draupada ! no Viráta ! no glad face
   Of Dhrishtaketu ! no Shikandina,
   Prince of Panchála, nor his princely boys !

Nor Abhimanyu the unconquerable!
President Gods of heaven! I see not here
Radha's bright son, nor Yudhamanyu,
Nor Uttamanjaso, his brother dear!
Where are those noble Maharashtra lords,
Rajahs and rajpoots, slain for love of me?
Dwell they in glory elsewhere, not yet seen?
If they be here, high Gods! and those with them
For whose sweet sakes I lived, here will I live,
Meek-hearted; but if such be not adjudged
Worthy, I am not worthy, nor my soul
Willing to rest without them.   Ah, I burn,
Now in glad heaven, with grief, bethinking me
Of those my mother's words, what time I poured
Death-water for my dead at Kurkshetra,—
" Pour for Prince Karna, Son!" but I wist not
His feet were as my mother's feet, his blood
Her blood, my blood.   O Gods! I did not know,—
Albeit Sakra's self had failed to break
Our battle, where *he* stood.   I crave to see
Surya's child, that glorious chief who fell
By Saryasáchi's hand, unknown of me;
And Bhíma! ah, my Bhíma! dearer far

Than life to me ; Arjuna, like a god,
Nakla and Sahadev, twin lords of war,
With tenderest Draupadí ! Show me those souls !
I cannot tarry where I have them not.
Bliss is not blissful, just and mighty Ones !
Save if I rest beside them.   Heaven is there
Where Love and Faith make heaven.   Let me go !'

" And answer made the hearkening heavenly Ones :
' Go, if it seemeth good to thee, dear Son !
The King of gods commands we do thy will.'

" So saying [the Bard went on] Dharma's own voice
Gave ordinance, and from the shining bands
A golden Deva glided, taking hest
To guide the king there where his kinsmen were.
So wended these, the holy angel first,
And in his steps the king, close following.
Together passed they through the gates of pearl,
Together heard them close ; then to the left
Descending, by a path evil and dark,
Hard to be traversed, rugged, entered they
The ' SINNERS' ROAD.'   The tread of sinful feet

Matted the thick thorns carpeting its slope ;
The smell of sin hung foul on them; the mire
About their roots was trampled filth of flesh
Horrid with rottenness, and splashed with gore
Curdling in crimson puddles; where there buzzed
And sucked and settled creatures of the swamp,
Hideous in wing and sting, gnat-clouds and flies,
With moths, toads, newts, and snakes red-gulleted,
And livid, loathsome worms, writhing in slime
Forth from skull-holes and scalps and tumbled bones.
A burning forest shut the roadside in
On either hand, and 'mid its crackling boughs
Perched ghastly birds, or flapped amongst the flames,—
Vultures and kites and crows,—with brazen plumes
And beaks of iron ; and these grisly fowl
Screamed to the shrieks of Prets, lean, famished ghosts,
Featureless, eyeless, having pin-point mouths,
Hungering, but hard to fill,—all swooping down
To gorge upon the meat of wicked ones ;
Whereof the limbs disparted, trunks and heads,
Offal and marrow, littered all the way.
By such a path the king passed, sore afeared
If he had known of fear, for the air stank

With carrion stench, sickly to breathe; and lo!
Presently 'thwart the pathway foamed a flood
Of boiling waves, rolling down corpses.   This
They crossed, and then the Asipatra wood
Spread black in sight, whereof the undergrowth
Was sword-blades, spitting, every blade, some wretch;
All around poison trees; and next to this,
Strewn deep with fiery sands, an awful waste,
Wherethrough the wicked toiled with blistering feet,
'Midst rocks of brass, red hot, which scorched, and pools
Of bubbling pitch that gulfed them.   Last the gorge
Of Kutashála Mali,—frightful gate
Of utmost Hell, with utmost horrors filled.
Deadly and nameless were the plagues seen there;
Which when the monarch reached, nigh overborne
By terrors and the reek of tortured flesh,
Unto the angel spake he: 'Whither goes
This hateful road, and where be they I seek,
Yet find not?'   Answer made the heavenly One:
'Hither, great King, it was commanded me
To bring thy steps.   If thou be'st overborne,
It is commanded that I lead thee back
To where the Gods wait.   Wilt thou turn and mount?'

" Then (O thou Son of Bhárat!) Yudhishthir
   Turned heavenward his face, so was he moved
   With horror and the hanging stench, and spent
   By toil of that black travel.   But his feet
   Scarce one stride measured, when about the place
   Pitiful accents rang: ' Alas, sweet King!—
   Ah, saintly Lord!—Ah, Thou that hast attained
   Place with the Blessèd, Pandu's offspring!—pause
   A little while, for love of us who cry!
   Nought can harm *thee* in all this baneful place ;
   But at thy coming there 'gan blow a breeze
   Balmy and soothing, bringing us relief.
   O Pritha's son, mightiest of men ! we breathe
   Glad breath again to see thee; we have peace
   One moment in our agonies.   Stay here
   One moment more, Bhárata's child !   Go not,
   Thou Victor of the Kurus !   Being here,
   Hell softens and our bitter pains relax.'

" These pleadings, wailing all around the place,
   Heard the King Yudhishthira,—words of woe
   Humble and eager; and compassion seized
   His lordly mind.   ' Poor souls unknown !' he sighed,

And hellwards turned anew ; for what those were,

Whence such beseeching voices, and of whom,

That son of Pandu wist not,—only wist

That all the noxious murk was filled with forms,

Shadowy, in anguish, crying grace of him.

Wherefore he called aloud, ' Who speaks with me ?

What do ye here, and what things suffer ye ? '

Then from the black depth piteously there came

Answers of whispered suffering : ' Karna I,

O King ! ' and yet another, ' O my Liege,

Thy Bhíma speaks ! ' and then a voice again,

' I am Arjuna, Brother ! ' and again,

' Nakla is here and Sahadev ! ' and last

A moan of music from the darkness sighed,

' Draupadí cries to thee ! '   Thereat broke forth

The monarch's spirit,—knowing so the sound

Of each familiar voice,—' What doom is this ?

What have my well-belovèd wrought to earn

Death with the damned, or life loathlier than death

In Narak's midst ?   Hath Karna erred so deep,

Bhíma, Arjuna, or the glorious twins,

Or she, the slender-waisted, sweetest, best,

My princess,—that Duryodhana should sit

Peaceful in Paradise with all his crew,

Throned by Mahendra and the shining gods ?

How should these fail of bliss, and he attain ?

What were their sins to his, their splendid faults ?

For if they slipped, it was in virtue's way

Serving good laws, performing holy rites,

Boundless in gifts and faithful to the death.

These be their well-known voices !   Are ye here,

Souls I loved best ?   Dream I, belike, asleep,

Or rave I, maddened with accursèd sights

And death-reeks of this hellish air ? '

                                   " Thereat

For pity and for pain the king waxed wroth.

That soul fear could not shake, nor trials tire,

Burned terrible with tenderness, the while

His eyes searched all the gloom, his planted feet

Stood fast in the mid horrors.   Well-nigh, then,

He cursed the gods ; well-nigh that steadfast mind

Broke from its faith in virtue.   But he stayed

Th' indignant passion, softly speaking this

Unto the angel : ' Go to those thou serv'st ;

Tell them I come not thither.   Say I stand

Here in the throat of hell, and here will bide—
Nay, if I perish—while my well-belov'd
Win ease and peace by any pains of mine.'

" Whereupon, nought replied the shining One,
But straight repaired unto the upper light,
Where Sákra sate above the gods, and spake
Before the gods the message of the king."

———————

" Afterward what befell ? " the prince inquired.

" Afterward, Princely One ! " replied the Sage,
" At hearing and at knowing that high deed
(Great Yudhishthira braving hell for love),
The Presences of Paradise uprose,
Each Splendour in his place,—god Sákra chief;
Together rose they, and together stepped
Down from their thrones, treading the nether road
Where Yudhishthira tarried. Sákra led
The shining van, and Dharma, Lord of laws,
Paced glorious next. O Son of Bhárata,

While that celestial company came down—
Pure as the white stars sweeping through the sky,
And brighter than their brilliance—look! Hell's shades
Melted before them; warm gleams drowned the gloom;
Soft, lovely scenes rolled over the ill sights;
Peace calmed the cries of torment; in its bed
The boiling river shrank, quiet and clear;
The Asipatra Vana—awful wood—
Blossomed with colours; all those cruel blades,
And dreadful rocks, and piteous scattered wreck
Of writhing bodies, where the king had passed,
Vanished as dreams fade.   Cool and fragrant went
A wind before their faces, as these Gods
Drew radiant to the presence of the king,—
Maruts; and Vasus eight, who shine and serve
Round Indra; Rudras; Aswins; and those Six
Immortal Lords of light beyond our light,
Th' Adityas; Saddhyas; Siddhas,—those were there,
With angels, saints, and habitants of heaven,
Smiling resplendent round the steadfast prince.

" Then spake the God of gods these gracious words
To Yudhishthira, standing in that place :—

" ' King Yudhishthira! O thou long-armed Lord,

This is enough! All heaven is glad of thee.

It is enough! Come, thou most blessèd one,

Unto thy peace, well-gained. Lay now aside

Thy loving wrath, and hear the speech of Heaven.

It is appointed that all kings see hell.

The reckonings for the life of men are twain:

Of each man's righteous deeds a tally true,

A tally true of each man's evil deeds.

Who hath wrought little right, to him is paid

A little bliss in Swarga, then the woe

Which purges; who much right hath wrought, from

    him

The little ill by lighter pains is cleansed,

And then the joys. Sweet is peace after pain,

And bitter pain which follows peace; yet they,

Who sorely sin, taste of the heaven they miss,

And they that suffer quit their debt at last.

Lo! We have loved thee, laying hard on thee

Grievous assaults of soul, and this black road.

Bethink thee: by a semblance once, dear Son!

Drona thou didst beguile; and once, dear Son!

Semblance of hell hath so thy sin assoiled,

Which passeth with these shadows. Even thus
Thy Bhíma came a little space t' account,
Draupadí, Krishna,—all whom thou didst love,
Never again to lose! Come, First of Men!
These be delivered and their quittance made.
Also the princes, son of Bhárata!
Who fell beside thee fighting, have attained.
Come thou to see! Karna, whom thou didst mourn,—
That mightiest archer, master in all wars,—
He hath attained, shining as doth the sun;
Come thou and see! Grieve no more, King of Men!
Whose love helped them and thee, and hath its meed.
Rajas and maharajahs, warriors, aids,—
All thine are thine for ever. Krishna waits
To greet thee coming, 'companied by gods,
Seated in heaven, from toils and conflicts saved.
Son! there is golden fruit of noble deeds,
Of prayer, alms, sacrifice. The most just Gods
Keep thee thy place above the highest saints,
Where thou shalt sit, divine, compassed about
With royal souls in bliss, as Hari sits;
Seeing Mándháta crowned, and Bhagirath,
Daushyanti, Bhárata, with all thy line.

Now therefore wash thee in this holy stream,

Gunga's pure fount, whereof the bright waves bless

All the Three Worlds.   It will so change thy flesh

To likeness of th' immortal, thou shalt leave

Passions and aches and tears behind thee there.'

" And when the awful Sákra thus had said,

  Lo! Dharma spake,—th' embodied Lord of Right:

"' Bho! bho! I am well pleased!   Hail to thee, Chief!

  Worthy, and wise, and firm.   Thy faith is full,

  Thy virtue, and thy patience, and thy truth,

  And thy self-mastery.   Thrice I put thee, King!

  Unto the trial.   In the Dwaita wood,

  The day of sacrifice,—then thou stood'st fast;

  Next, on thy brethren's death and Draupadí's,

  When, as a dog, I followed thee, and found

  Thy spirit constant to the meanest friend.

  Here was the third and sorest touchstone, Son!

  That thou shouldst hear thy brothers cry in hell,

  And yet abide to help them.   Pritha's child,

  We love thee!   Thou art fortunate and pure,

  Past trials now.   Thou art approved, and they

Thou lov'st have tasted hell only a space,

Not meriting to suffer more than when

An evil dream doth come, and Indra's beam

Ends it with radiance—as this vision ends.

It is appointed that all flesh see death,

And therefore thou hast borne the passing pangs,

Briefest for thee, and brief for those of thine,—

Bhíma the faithful, and the valiant twins

Nakla and Sahadev, and those great hearts

Karna, Arjuna, with thy princess dear,

Draupadí.   Come, thou best-belovèd Son,

Blessed of all thy line!   Bathe in this stream,—

It is great Gunga, flowing through Three Worlds.'

" Thus high-accosted, the rejoicing king

(Thy ancestor, O Liege!) proceeded straight

Unto that river's brink, which floweth pure

Through the Three Worlds, mighty, and sweet, and

        praised.

There, being bathed, the body of the king

Put off its mortal, coming up arrayed

In grace celestial, washed from soils of sin,

From passion, pain, and change.   So, hand in hand

With brother-gods, glorious went Yudhishthir,

Lauded by softest minstrelsy, and songs

Of unknown music, where those heroes stood—

The princes of the Pandavas, his kin—

And lotus-eyed and lovliest Draupadí,

Waiting to greet him, gladdening and glad.

FROM THE "SAUPTIKA PARVA" OF THE MAHÁBHÁRATA,

OR

"NIGHT OF SLAUGHTER."

———0———

To Narayen, Best of Lords, be glory given,
To great Saraswati, the Queen in Heaven;
Unto Vyása, too, be paid his meed,
So shall this story worthily proceed.

" Those vanquished warriors then," Sanjaya said,
" Fled southwards; and, near sunset, past the tents,
Unyoked; abiding close in fear and rage.
There was a wood beyond the camp,—untrod,
Quiet,—and in its leafy harbour lay
The Princes, some among them bleeding still
From spear and arrow-gashes; all sore-spent,

Fetching faint breath, and fighting o'er again
In thought that battle. But there came the noise
Of Pandavas pursuing,—fierce and loud
Outcries of victory—whereat those chiefs
Sullenly rose, and yoked their steeds again,
Driving due east; and eastward still they drave
Under the night, till drouth and desperate toil
Stayed horse and man; then took they lair again,
The panting horses, and the Warriors, wroth
With chilled wounds, and the death-stroke of their
  King.

"Now were they come, my Prince," Sanjaya said,
" Unto a jungle thick with stems, whereon
The tangled creepers coiled; here entered they—
Watering their horses at a stream—and pushed
Deep in the thicket. Many a beast and bird
Sprang startled at their feet; the long grass stirred
With serpents creeping off; the woodland flowers
Shook where the pea-fowl hid, and, where frogs plunged,
The swamp rocked all its reeds and lotus-buds.
A banian-tree, with countless dropping boughs
Earth-rooted, spied they, and beneath its aisles

A pool; hereby they stayed, tethering their steeds,
And dipping water, made the evening prayer.

" But when the 'Day-maker' sank in the west
  And Night descended—gentle, soothing Night,
  Who comforts all, with silver splendour decked
  Of stars and constellations, and soft folds
  Of velvet darkness drawn—then those wild things
  Which roam in darkness woke, wandering afoot
  Under the gloom.   Horrid the forest grew
  With roar, and yelp, and yell, around that place
  Where Kripa, Kritavarman, and the son
  Of Drona lay, beneath the banian-tree;
  Full many a piteous passage instancing
  In their lost battle-day of dreadful blood;
  Till sleep fell heavy on the wearied lids
  Of Bhoja's child and Kripa.   Then these Lords—
  To princely life and silken couches used—
  Sought on the bare earth slumber, spent and sad,
  As houseless outcasts lodge.

                      " But„ Oh, my King!
There came no sleep to Drona's angry son,

Great Aswatthâman.   As a snake lies coiled

And hisses, breathing, so his panting breath

Hissed rage and hatred round him, while he lay,

Chin uppermost, arm-pillowed, with fierce eyes

Roving the wood, and seeing sightlessly.

Thus chanced it that his wandering glances turned

Into the fig-tree's shadows, where there perched

A thousand crows, thick-roosting, on its limbs;

Some nested, some on branchlets, deep asleep,

Heads under wings—all fearless; nor, O Prince!

Had Aswatthâman more than marked the birds,

When, lo! there fell out of the velvet night,

Silent and terrible, an eagle-owl,

With wide, soft, deadly, dusky wings, and eyes

Flame-coloured, and long claws, and dreadful beak;

Like a winged sprite, or great Garood himself.

Offspring of Bhârata! it lighted there

Upon the banian's bough; hooted, but low,

The fury smothering in its throat;—then fell

With murderous beak and claws upon those crows,

Rending the wings from this, the legs from that,

From some the heads, of some ripping the crops;

Till, tens and scores, the fowl rained down to earth

Bloody and plucked, and all the ground waxed black
With piled crow-carcases; whilst the great owl
Hooted for joy of vengeance, and again
Spread the wide, deadly, dusky wings.

"Up sprang

The son of Drona: 'Lo! this owl,' quoth he,
'Teacheth me wisdom; lo! one slayeth so
Insolent foes asleep.   The Pandu Lords
Are all too strong in arms by day to kill;
They triumph, being many.   Yet I swore
Before the King, my Father, I would "kill"
And "kill"—even as a foolish fly should swear
To quench a flame.   It scorched, and I shall die
If I dare open battle; but by art
Men vanquish fortune and the mightiest odds.
If there be two ways to a wise man's wish,
Yet only one way sure, he taketh this;
And if it be an evil way, condemned
For Brahmans, yet the Kshattriya may do
What vengeance bids against his foes.   Our foes,
The Pandavas, are furious, treacherous, base,
Halting at nothing; and how say the wise

In holy Shasters ?—" Wounded, wearied, fed,
Or fasting; sleeping, waking, setting forth,
Or new arriving; slay thine enemies;"
And so again, " At midnight when they sleep,
Dawn when they watch not; noon if leaders fall;
Eve, should they scatter; all the times and hours
Are times and hours fitted for killing foes." '

" So did the son of Drona steel his soul
　To break upon the sleeping Pandu chiefs
　And slay them in the darkness.　Being set
　On this unlordly deed, and clear in scheme,
　He from their slumbers roused the warriors twain,
　Kripa and Kritavarman."

THE MORNING PRAYER.

—o—

OUR Lord the Prophet (peace to him!) doth write—
Súrah the Seventeenth, intituled "Night"—
" Pray at the noon; pray at the sinking sun;
In night-time pray; but most when night is done;
For daybreak's prayer is surely borne on high
By angels, changing guard within the sky;"
And in another place:—" Dawn's prayer is more
Than the wide world, with all its treasured store."

Therefore the Faithful, when the growing light
Gives to discern a black hair from a white,
Haste to the mosque, and, bending Mecca-way,
Recite *Al-Fátihah* while 'tis scarce yet day:
" *Praise be to Allah—Lord of all that live:*
Merciful King and Judge ! To Thee we give

Worship and honour !   Succour us, and guide
Where those have walked who rest Thy throne beside :
The way of Peace ; the way of truthful speech ;
The way of Righteousness.   So we beseech."
He that saith this, before the East is red,
A hundred prayers of Azan hath he said.

Hear now a story of it—told, I ween,
For your souls' comfort by Jelal-ud-din,
In the great pages of the Mesnevî;
For therein, plain and certain, shall ye see
How precious is the prayer at break of day
In Allah's ears, and in his sight alway
How sweet are reverence and gentleness
Shown to his creatures.   Àli (whom I bless !)
The son of Abu Talib—he surnamed
"Lion of God," in many battles famed,
The cousin of our Lord the Prophet (grace
Be his !)—uprose betimes one morn, to pace—
As he was wont—unto the mosque, wherein
Our Lord (bliss live with him !) watched to begin
Al-Fátihah.   Darkling was the sky, and strait
The lane between the city and mosque-gate,

By rough stones broken and deep pools of rain;

And there through toilfully, with steps of pain,

Leaning upon his staff an old Jew went

To synagogue, on pious errand bent:

For those be " People of the Book,"—and some

Are chosen of Allah's will, who have not come

Unto full light of wisdom.   Therefore he

Àli—the Caliph of proud days to be—

Knowing this good old man, and why he stirred

Thus early, e'er the morning mills were heard,

Out of his nobleness and grace of soul

Would not thrust past, though the Jew blocked the

    whole

Breadth of the lane, slow-hobbling.   So they went,

That ancient first; and in soft discontent,

After him Àli—noting how the sun

Flared nigh, and fearing prayer might be begun;

Yet no command upraising, no harsh cry

To stand aside;—because the dignity

Of silver hairs is much, and morning praise

Was precious to the Jew, too.   Thus their ways

Wended the pair; Great Àli, sad and slow,

Following the greybeard, while the East, a-glow,

Blazed with bright spears of gold athwart the blue,

And the Muezzin's call came "*Illahu !*

Allah-il-Allah !"

       In the mosque, our Lord

(On whom be peace!) stood by the Mehrab-board

In act to bow, and *Fâtihah* forth to say.

But as his lips moved, some strong hand did lay

Over his mouth a palm invisible,

So that no voice on the Assembly fell.

"*Ya ! Rabbi 'lalamîna*" thrice he tried

To read, and thrice the sound of reading died,

Stayed by this unseen touch. Thereat amazed

Our Lord Muhammed turned, arose, and gazed;

And saw—alone of those within the shrine—

A splendid Presence, with large eyes divine

Beaming, and golden pinions folded down,

Their speed still tokened by the fluttered gown.

GABRIEL he knew, the spirit who doth stand

Chief of the Sons of Heav'n, at God's right hand:

"Gabriel! why stayest thou me?" the Prophet said,

"Since at this hour the *Fâtihah* should be read."

But the bright Presence, smiling, pointed where
Àli towards the outer gate drew near,
Upon the threshold shaking off his shoes
And giving "alms of entry," as men use.
"Yea!" spake th' Archangel, "sacred is the sound
Of morning-praise, and worth the world's wide round,
Though earth were pearl and silver; therefore I
Stayed thee, Muhammed, in the act to cry,
Lest Àli, tarrying in the lane, should miss,
For his good deed, its blessing and its bliss."

Thereat th' Archangel vanished :—and our Lord
Read *Fâtihah* forth beneath the Mehrab-board.

PROVERBIAL WISDOM

FROM THE

SHLOKAS OF THE HITOPADESA.

Dedication

(*TO FIRST EDITION*).

To you, dear Wife—to whom beside so well ? —
True Counsellor and tried, at every shift,
I bring my " Book of Counsels :" let it tell
Largeness of love by littleness of gift :

And take this growth of foreign skies from me,
(A scholar's thanks for gentle help in toil,)
Whose leaf, " though dark," like Milton's Hæmony,
" Bears a bright golden flower, if not in this soil."

April 9, 1861.

PREFACE

TO THE "BOOK OF GOOD COUNSELS."

——*o*——

THE *Hitopadeśa* is a work of high antiquity and extended popularity. The prose is doubtless as old as our own era; but the intercalated verses and proverbs compose a selection from writings of an age extremely remote. The *Mahábhárata* and the textual *Veds* are of those quoted; to the first of which Professor M. Williams (in his admirable edition of the *Nala*, 1860) assigns the modest date of 350 B.C., while he claims for the *Rig-Veda* an antiquity as high as 1300 B.C. The *Hitopadeśa* may thus be fairly styled "The Father of all Fables;" for from its numerous translations have probably come Esop and Pilpay, and in latter days *Reineke Fuchs.* Originally compiled in Sanskrit, it was rendered, by order of Nushirván, in the sixth century A.D., into Persic. From the Persic it passed, A.D. 850, into the Arabic, and thence into Hebrew and Greek. In its own land it obtained as wide a circulation. The Emperor Akbar, impressed with the wisdom of its maxims and the ingenuity of its apologues, commended the work of translating it to his own Vizier, Abdul Fazel. That Minister accordingly put the book into a familiar style, and published it with explanations, under the title of the *Criterion of Wisdom.* The Emperor had also suggested the abridgment of the long series of shlokes which here and there interrupt the narrative, and the Vizier found this advice sound, and followed it, like the present Translator. To this day, in India, the *Hitopadeśa,* under its own or other names (as the *Anvári Suhaili*), retains the delighted attention of young and old, and has some representative in all the Indian vernaculars. A selection from the metrical Sanskrit proverbs and maxims is here given.

PROVERBIAL WISDOM

FROM THE

SHLOKAS OF THE HITOPADEŚA.

———o———

This Book of Counsel read, and you shall see,
Fair speech and Sanskrit lore, and Policy.

" Wise men, holding wisdom highest, scorn delights,
    more false than fair;
  Daily live as if Death's fingers twined already in thy
    hair!

" Truly, richer than all riches, better than the best of
    gain,
  Wisdom is ; unbought, secure—once won, none loseth
    her again.

P

"Bringing dark things into daylight, solving doubts
    that vex the mind,
  Like an open eye is Wisdom—he that hath her not
    is blind."

———

"Childless art thou? dead thy children? leaving thee
    to want and doole?
  Less thy misery than his is, who lives father to a fool."

"One wise son makes glad his father, forty fools avail
    him not:
  One moon silvers all that darkness which the silly
    stars did dot."

"Ease and health, obeisant children, wisdom, and a fair-
    voiced wife—
  Thus, great King! are counted up the five felicities
    of life.

"For the son the sire is honoured; though the bow-cane
    bendeth true,
  Let the strained string crack in using, and what ser-
    vice shall it do?"

" That which will not be, will not be—and what is to
  be, will be :

Why not drink this easy physic, antidote of misery ? "

" Nay ! but faint not, idly sighing, ' Destiny is mightiest,'
Sesamum holds oil in plenty, but it yieldeth none
  unpressed."

" Ah ! it is the Coward's babble, ' Fortune taketh, Fortune gave ;'
Fortune ! rate her like a master, and she serves thee
  like a slave."

" Two-fold is the life we live in—Fate and Will together
  run :
Two wheels bear life's chariot onward—Will it move
  on only one ? "

" Look ! the clay dries into iron, but the potter moulds
  the clay :
Destiny to-day is master—Man was master yester-
  day."

"Worthy ends come not by wishing. Wouldst thou?
    Up, and win it, then!
  While the hungry lion slumbers, not a deer comes to
    his den."

———

"Silly glass, in splendid settings, something of the gold
    may gain;
  And in company of wise ones, fools to wisdom may
    attain."

"Labours spent on the unworthy, of reward the
    labourer balk;
  Like the parrot, teach the heron twenty words, he will
    not talk."

———

"Ah! a thousand thoughts of sorrow, and a hundred
    things of dread,
  By the fools unheeded, enter day by day the wise
    man's head."

"Of the day's impending dangers, Sickness, Death, and
    Misery,
  One will be; the wise man, waking, ponders which
    that one will be."

" Good things come not out of bad things; wisely leave
  a longed-for ill.

Nectar being mixed with poison serves no purpose
  but to kill."

———

"Give to poor men, son of Kûnti—on the wealthy
  waste not wealth;

Good are simples for the sick man, good for nought
  to him in health."

———

" Be his Scripture-learning wondrous, yet the cheat will
  be a cheat;

Be her pasture ne'er so bitter, yet the cow's milk will
  taste sweet."

———

" Trust not water, trust not weapons; trust not clawed
  nor horned things;

Neither give thy soul to women, nor thy life to Sons
  of Kings."

———

" Look! the Moon, the silver roamer, from whose splendour darkness flies,

With his starry cohorts marching, like a crowned king,
  through the skies:

All his grandeur, all his glory, vanish in the Dragon's
    jaw;

What is written on the forehead, that will be, and
    nothing more."

———

"Counsel in danger; of it
    Unwarned, be nothing begun;
But nobody asks a Prophet,
    Shall the risk of a dinner be run?"

———

"Avarice begetteth anger; blind desires from her
    begin;
A right fruitful mother is she of a countless spawn
    of sin."

———

"Be second and not first!—the share's the same
If all go well. If not, the Head's to blame."

———

"Passion will be Slave or Mistress: follow her, she
    brings to woe;
Lead her, 'tis the way to Fortune. Choose the path
    that thou wilt go."

" When the time of trouble cometh, friends may ofttimes
    irk us most:
For the calf at milking-hour the mother's leg is tying-
    post."

———

" In good-fortune not elated, in ill-fortune not dismayed,
Ever eloquent in council, never in the fight affrayed,
Proudly emulous of honour, steadfastly on wisdom set;
These six virtues in the nature of a noble soul are met.
Whoso hath them, gem and glory of the three wide
    worlds is he;
Happy mother she that bore him, she who nursed him
    on her knee."

———

" Small things wax exceeding mighty, being cunningly
    combined;
Furious elephants are fastened with a rope of grass-
    blades twined."

" Let the household hold together, though the house be
    ne'er so small;
Strip the rice-husk from the rice-grain, and it groweth
    not at all."

" Sickness, anguish, bonds, and woe
  Spring from wrongs wrought long ago."

———

" Keep wealth for want, but spend it for thy wife,
  And wife, and wealth, and all, to guard thy life."

———

" Death, that must come, comes nobly when we give
  Our wealth, and life, and all, to make men live."

———

"Floating on his fearless pinions, lost amid the noon-
    day skies,
  Even thence the Eagle's vision kens the carcass where
    it lies;
  But the hour that comes to all things comes unto the
    Lord of Air,
  And he rushes, madly blinded, to die helpless in the
    snare."

———

  Bar thy door not to the stranger, be he friend or be
    he foe,
  For the tree will shade the woodman while his axe
    doth lay it low.

Greeting fair, and room to rest in; fire, and water from
 the well—
Simple gifts—are given freely in the house where
 good men dwell;—

Young, or bent with many winters; rich, or poor,
 whate'er thy guest,
Honour him for thine own honour—better is he than
 the best.

"Pity them that crave thy pity: who art thou to stint
 thy hoard,
 When the holy moon shines equal on the leper and
 the lord?"

When thy gate is roughly fastened, and the asker
 turns away,
Thence he bears thy good deeds with him, and his
 sins on thee doth lay.

In the house the husband ruleth; men the Brahman
 "master" call;
Agni is the Twice-born's Master—but the guest is
 lord of all.

" He who does and thinks no wrong—
He who suffers, being strong—
He whose harmlessness men know—
Unto Swarga such doth go."

———

" In the land where no wise men are, men of little wit
are lords;
And the castor-oil's a tree, where no tree else its shade
affords."

———

" Foe is friend, and friend is foe,
As our actions make them so."

" That friend only is the true friend who abides when
trouble comes;
That man only is the brave man who can bear the
battle-drums;
Words are wind; deed proveth promise: he who
helps at need is kin;
And the leal wife is loving though the husband lose
or win."

" Friend and kinsman—more their meaning than the
    idle-hearted mind ;
Many a friend can prove unfriendly, many a kinsman
    less than kind :
He who shares his comrade's portion, be he beggar,
    be he lord,
Comes as truly, comes as duly, to the battle as the
    board—
Stands before the king to succour, follows to the pile
    to sigh—
He is friend, and he is kinsman ; less would make the
    name a lie."

———

" Stars gleam, lamps flicker, friends foretell of fate ;
The fated sees, knows, hears them—all too late."

———

" Absent, flatterers' tongues are daggers—present, softer
    than the silk ;
Shun them ! 'tis a draught of poison hidden under
    harmless milk ;

Shun them when they promise little! Shun them
    when they promise much!
For enkindled, charcoal burneth—cold, it doth defile
    the touch."

    " In years, or moons, or half-moons three,
      Or in three days—suddenly,
      Knaves are shent—true men go free."

" Anger comes to noble natures, but leaves there no
    strife or storm:
Plunge a lighted torch beneath it, and the ocean grows
    not warm."

" Noble hearts are golden vases—close the bond true
    metals make;
Easily the smith may weld them, harder far it is to
    break.
Evil hearts are earthen vessels—at a touch they crack
    a-twain,
And what craftsman's ready cunning can unite the
    shards again ? "

" Good men's friendships may be broken, yet abide they

friends at heart ;

Snap the stem of Luxmee's lotus, but its fibres will

not part."

———

" One foot goes, and one foot stands,

When the wise man leaves his lands."

———

" Over-love of home were weakness; wheresoe'er the

hero come,

Stalwart arm and steadfast spirit find or make for

him a home.

Little recks the awless lion where his hunting jungles

lie—

When he enters them be certain that a royal prey

shall die."

———

" Very feeble folk are poor folk; money lost takes wit

away :

All their doings fail like runnels, wasting through the

summer day."

Wealth is friends, home, father, brother—title to re-
   spect and fame;
Yea, and wealth is held for wisdom—that it should
   be so is shame."

"Home is empty to the childless; hearts to those who
   friends deplore:
Earth unto the idle-minded; and the three worlds to
   the poor."

"Say the sages, nine things name not: Age, domestic
   joys and woes,
Counsel, sickness, shame, alms, penance; neither
   Poverty disclose.
Better for the proud of spirit, death, than life with
   losses told;
Fire consents to be extinguished, but submits not to
   be cold."

"As Age doth banish beauty,
   As moonlight dies in gloom,
As Slavery's menial duty
   Is Honour's certain tomb;

As Hari's name and Hara's
    Spoken, charm sin away,
So Poverty can surely
    A hundred virtues slay."

" Half-known knowledge, present pleasure purchased
        with a future woe,
    And to taste the salt of service—greater griefs no
        man can know."

" All existence is not equal, and all living is not
        life ;
    Sick men live ; and he who, banished, pines for chil-
        dren, home, and wife ;
    And the craven-hearted eater of another's leavings
        lives,
    And the wretched captive, waiting for the word of
        doom, survives ;
    But they bear an anguished body, and they draw a
        deadly breath ;
    And life cometh to them only on the happy day of
        death."

" Golden gift, serene Contentment ! have thou that,
    and all is had ;
Thrust thy slipper on, and think thee that the earth
    is leather-clad."

" All is known, digested, tested ; nothing new is left to
    learn
When the soul, serene, reliant, Hope's delusive dreams
    can spurn."

" Hast thou never watched, a-waiting till the great
    man's door unbarred ?
Didst thou never linger parting, saying many a sad
    last word ?
Spak'st thou never word of folly, one light thing thou
    would'st recall ?
Rare and noble hath thy life been ! fair thy fortune
    did befall ! "

" True Religion !—'tis not blindly prating what the
    gurus prate,
But to love, as God hath loved them, all things, be
    they small or great ;

And true bliss is when a sane mind doth a healthy
body fill;
And true knowledge is the knowing what is good and
what is ill."

———

" Poisonous though the tree of life be, two fair blossoms
grow thereon:
One, the company of good men; and sweet songs of
Poets, one."

———

" Give, and it shall swell thy getting; give, and thou
shalt safer keep:
Pierce the tank-wall; or it yieldeth, when the water
waxeth deep."

" When the miser hides his treasure in the earth, he
doeth well;
For he opens up a passage that his soul may sink to
hell."

" He whose coins are kept for counting, not to barter
nor to give,
Breathe he like a blacksmith's bellows, yet in truth
he doth not live."

Q

" Gifts, bestowed with words of kindness, making giving
    doubly dear :

Wisdom, deep, complete, benignant, of all arrogancy
    clear ;

Valour, never yet forgetful of sweet Mercy's pleading
    prayer ;

Wealth, and scorn of wealth to spend it—oh ! but
    these be virtues rare ! "

———

" Sentences of studied wisdom, nought avail they un-
    applied ;

Though the blind man hold a lantern, yet his foot-
    steps stray aside."

———

" Would'st thou know whose happy dwelling Fortune
    entereth unknown ?

His, who careless of her favour, standeth fearless in
    his own ;

His, who for the vague to-morrow barters not the
    sure to-day—

Master of himself, and sternly steadfast to the right-
    ful way :

Very mindful of past service, valiant, faithful, true of
heart—
Unto such comes Lakshmi smiling—comes, and will
not lightly part."

———

"Be not haughty, being wealthy; droop not, having
lost thine all;
Fate doth play with mortal fortunes as a girl doth
toss her ball."

"Worldly friendships, fair but fleeting; shadows of the
clouds at noon;
Women, youth, new corn, and riches; these be pleasures passing soon."

———

"For thy bread be not o'er thoughtful—Heav'n for all
hath taken thought:
When the babe is born, the sweet milk to the mother's
breast is brought.

"He who gave the swan her silver, and the hawk her
plumes of pride,
And his purples to the peacock—He will verily
provide."

"Though for good ends, waste not on wealth a minute ;
Mud may be wiped, but wise men plunge not in it."

———

" Brunettes, and the Banyan's shadow,
    Well-springs, and a brick-built wall,
  Are all alike cool in the summer,
    And warm in the winter—all."

———

" Ah ! the gleaming, glancing arrows of a lovely woman's
    eye !
  Feathered with her jetty lashes, perilous they pass
    thee by :
  Loosed at venture from the black bows of her arching
    brow, they part,
  All too penetrant and deadly for an undefended
    heart."

———

" Beautiful the Koïl seemeth for the sweetness of his
    song,
  Beautiful the world esteemeth pious souls for patience
    strong ;

Homely features lack not favour when true wisdom
 they reveal,
And a wife is fair and honoured while her heart is
 firm and leal."

———

" Friend! gracious word!—the heart to tell is ill able
Whence came to men this jewel of a syllable."

———

  " Whoso for greater quits small gain,
   Shall have his labour for his pain;
   The things unwon unwon remain,
   And what was won is lost again."

———

" Looking down on lives below them, men of little store
  are great;
Looking up to higher fortunes, hard to each man
  seems his fate."

" As a bride, unwisely wedded, shuns the cold caress of
  eld,
So, from coward souls and slothful, Lakshmi's favours
  turn repelled."

" Ease, ill-health, home-keeping, sleeping, woman-
    service, and content—
  In the path that leads to greatness these be six
    obstructions sent."

" Seeing how the soorma wasteth, seeing how the ant-
    hill grows,
  Little adding unto little—live, give, learn, as life-time
    goes."

" Drops of water falling, falling, falling, brim the chatty
    o'er ;
  Wisdom comes in little lessons—little gains make
    largest store."

        " Men their cunning schemes may spin—
          God knows who shall lose or win."

          ———

" Shoot a hundred shafts, the quarry lives and flies—
    not due to death ;
  When his hour is come, a grass-blade hath a point to
    stop his breath."

" Robes were none, nor oil of unction, when the King

of Beasts was crowned :

'Twas his own fierce roar proclaimed him, rolling all

the kingdom round."

———

" What but for their vassals,

Elephant and man—

Swing of golden tassels,

Wave of silken fan—

But for regal manner

That the ' Chattra ' brings,

Horse, and foot, and banner—

What would come of kings ? "

———

" At the work-time, asking wages—is it like a faithful

herd ?

When the work's done, grudging wages—is *that* acting

like a lord ? "

" Serve the Sun with sweat of body; starve thy maw

to feed the flame;

Stead thy lord with all thy service; to thy death go,

quit of blame."

" Many prayers for him are uttered whereon many a
 life relies;
 'Tis but one poor fool the fewer when the greedy
  jack-daw dies."

———

" Give thy Dog the merest mouthful, and he crouches
 at thy feet,
 Wags his tail, and fawns, and grovels, in his eagerness
  to eat;
 Bid the Elephant be feeding, and the best of fodder
  bring;
 Gravely — after much entreaty — condescends that
  mighty king."

———

" By their own deeds men go downward, by them men
 mount upward all,
 Like the diggers of a well, and like the builders of a
  wall."

———

" Rushes down the hill the crag, which upward 'twas so
 hard to roll:
 So to virtue slowly rises—so to vice quick sinks the
  soul."

" Who speaks unasked, or comes unbid,
Or counts on service—will be chid."

———

" Wise, modest, constant, ever close at hand,
Not weighing but obeying all command,
Such servant by a Monarch's throne may stand."

———

" Pitiful, who fearing failure, therefore no beginning
makes,
Why forswear a daily dinner for the chance of
stomach-aches ? "

———

" Nearest to the King is dearest, be thy merit low or
high ;
Women, creeping plants, and princes, twine round
that which groweth nigh."

———

" Pearls are dull in leaden settings, but the setter is to
blame ;
. Glass will glitter like the ruby, dulled with dust—are
they the same ? "

" And a fool may tread on jewels, setting in his turban
  glass;
  Yet, at selling, gems are gems, and fardels but for
  fardels pass."

———

" Horse and weapon, lute and volume, man and woman,
  gift of speech,
  Have their uselessness or uses in the one who owneth
  each."

———

" Not disparagement nor slander kills the spirit of the
  brave;
  Fling a torch down, upward ever burns the brilliant
  flame it gave."

———

" Wisdom from the mouth of children be it overpast of
  none;
  What man scorns to walk by lamplight in the absence
  of the sun ? "

———

" Strength serves Reason. Saith the Mahout, when he
  beats the brazen drum,
  ' Ho! ye elephants, to this work must your mighti-
  nesses come.' "

" Mighty natures war with mighty : when the raging
   tempests blow,
O'er the green rice harmless pass they, but they lay
   the palm-trees low."

" Narrow-necked to let out little, big of belly to keep
   much,
As a flagon is—the Vizier of a Sultan should be such."

———

" He who thinks a minute little, like a fool misuses
   more ;
He who counts a cowry nothing, being wealthy, will
   be poor."

———

" Brahmans, soldiers, these and kinsmen—of the three
   set none in charge :
For the Brahman, though you rack him, yields no
   treasure small or large ;
And the soldier, being trusted, writes his quittance
   with his sword,
And the kinsman cheats his kindred by the charter
   of the word ;

But a servant old in service, worse than any one is
   thought,
Who, by long-tried license fearless, knows his master's
   anger nought."

———

" Never tires the fire of burning, never wearies Death of
   slaying,
Nor the sea of drinking rivers, nor the bright-eyed of
   betraying."

———

   " From false friends that breed thee strife,
   From a house with serpents rife,
   Saucy slaves and brawling wife—
   Get thee forth, to save thy life."

———

" Teeth grown loose, and wicked-hearted ministers, and
   poison trees,
Pluck them by the roots together; 'tis the thing that
   giveth ease."

" Long-tried friends are friends to cleave to—never
   leave thou these i' the lurch:
What man shuns the fire as sinful for that once it
   burned a church?"

" Raise an evil soul to honour, and his evil bents
    remain;
Bind a cur's tail ne'er so straightly, yet it curleth up
    again."

" How, in sooth, should Trust and Honour change the
    evil nature's root ?
Though one watered them with nectar, poison-trees
    bear deadly fruit."

" Safe within the husk of silence guard the seed of
    counsel so
That it break not—being broken, then the seedling
    will not grow."

———

" Even as one who grasps a serpent, drowning in the
    bitter sea,
Death to hold and death to loosen—such is life's
    perplexity."

———

" Woman's love rewards the worthless—kings of knaves
    exalters be;
Wealth attends the selfish niggard, and the cloud rains
    on the sea."

" Many a knave wins fair opinions standing in fair
    company,
  As the sooty soorma pleases, lighted by a brilliant
    eye."

" Where the azure lotus blossoms, there the alligators
    hide;
  In the sandal-tree are serpents. Pain and pleasure
    live allied."

" Rich the sandal—yet no part is but a vile thing habits
    there;
  Snake and wasp haunt root and blossom; on the
    boughs sit ape and bear."

———

  " As a bracelet of crystal, once broke, is not mended
  So the favour of princes, once altered, is ended."

———

" Wrath of kings, and rage of lightning—both be very
    full of dread;
  But one falls on one man only—one strikes many
    victims dead."

" All men scorn the soulless coward who his manhood
 doth forget:

On a lifeless heap of ashes fearlessly the foot is set."

———

" Simple milk, when serpents drink it, straightway into
 venom turns ;

And a fool who heareth counsel all the wisdom of it
 spurns."

———

 " A modest manner fits a maid,
  And Patience is a man's adorning ;
  But brides may kiss, nor do amiss,
   And men may draw, at scathe and scorning."

———

" Serving narrow-minded masters dwarfs high natures
 to their size :

Seen before a convex mirror, elephants do show as
 mice."

———

" Elephants destroy by touching, snakes with point of
 tooth beguile ;

Kings by favour kill, and traitors murder with a fatal
 smile."

"Of the wife the lord is jewel, though no gems upon
   her beam;
Lacking him, she lacks adornment, howsoe'er her
   jewels gleam!"

"Hairs three-lakhs, and half-a-lakh hairs, on a man so
   many grow—
And so many years to Swarga shall the true wife
   surely go!"

"When the faithful wife, embracing tenderly her
   husband dead,
Mounts the blazing pyre beside him, as it were a
   bridal-bed;
Though his sins were twenty thousand, twenty thousand times o'er-told,
She shall bring his soul to splendour, for her love so
   large and bold."

———

"Counsel unto six ears spoken, unto all is notified:
When a King holds consultation, let it be with one
   beside."

"Sick men are for skilful leeches—prodigals for poison-
    ing—
Fools for teachers—and the man who keeps a secret,
    for a King."

———

" With gift, craft, promise, cause thy foe to yield;
  When these have failed thee, challenge him a-field."

———

" The subtle wash of waves do smoothly pass,
  But lay the tree as lowly as the grass."

———

"Ten true bowmen on a rampart fifty's onset may
    sustain;
Fortalices keep a country more than armies in the
    plain."

" Build it strong, and build it spacious, with an entry
    and retreat;
Store it well with wood and water, fill its garners full
    with wheat."

———

" Gems will no man's life sustain;
  Best of gold is golden grain."

R

" Hard it is to conquer nature: if a dog were made a
  King,
  'Mid the coronation trumpets he would gnaw his
  sandal-string."

———

" 'Tis no Council where no Sage is—'tis no Sage that
  fears not Law ;
  'Tis no Law which Truth confirms not—'tis no Truth
  which Fear can awe."

———

" Though base be the Herald, nor hinder nor let,
    For the mouth of a king is he;
  The sword may be whet, and the battle set,
    But the word of his message goes free."

" Better few and chosen fighters than of shaven-crowns
  a host,
  For in headlong flight confounded, with the base the
  brave are lost."

" Kind is kin, howe'er a stranger—kin unkind is stranger
  shown;
  Sores hurt, though the body breeds them—drugs
  relieve, though desert-grown."

" Betel - nut is bitter, hot, sweet, spicy, binding,
   alkaline—

A demulcent—an astringent—foe to evils intestine;

Giving to the breath a fragrance — to the lips a
   crimson red;

A detergent, and a kindler of Love's flame that lieth
   dead.

Praise the Gods for the good betel !—these be thirteen
   virtues given,

Hard to meet in one thing blended, even in their
   happy heaven."

———

" He is brave whose tongue is silent of the trophies of
   his sword;

He is great whose quiet bearing marks his greatness
   well assured."

" When the Priest, the Leech, the Vizier of a King his
   flatterers be,

Very soon the King will part with health, and wealth
   and piety."

" Merciless, or money-loving, deaf to counsel, false of
　　faith,
　Thoughtless, spiritless, or careless, changing course
　　with every breath,
　Or the man who scorns his rival—if a prince should
　　choose a foe,
　Ripe for meeting and defeating, certes he would
　　choose him so."

" By the valorous and unskilful great achievements
　　are not wrought;
　Courage, led by careful Prudence, unto highest ends
　　is brought."

" Grief kills gladness, winter summer, midnight-gloom
　　the light of day,
　Kindnesses ingratitude, and pleasant friends drive pain
　　away;
　Each ends each, but none of other surer conquerors
　　can be
　Than Impolicy of Fortune—of Misfortune Policy."

" Wisdom answers all who ask her, but a fool she can-
    not aid ;

Blind men in the faithful mirror see not their reflection
    made."

'' Where the Gods are, or thy Gúrú—in the face of Pain
    and Age,

Cattle, Brahmans, Kings, and Children—reverently
    curb thy rage."

" Oh, my Prince! on eight occasions prodigality is
    none—

In the solemn sacrificing, at the wedding of a son,

When the glittering treasure given makes the proud
    invader bleed,

Or its lustre bringeth comfort to the people in their
    need,

Or when kinsmen are to succour, or a worthy work
    to end,

Or to do a loved one honour, or to welcome back a
    friend."

" Truth, munificence, and valour, are the virtues of a
King;

Royalty, devoid of either, sinks to a rejected thing."

———

" Hold thy vantage !—alligators on the land make none
afraid;

And the lion's but a jackal who hath left his forest-
shade."

———

" The people are the lotus-leaves, their monarch is the
sun—

When he doth sink beneath the waves they vanish
every one.

When he doth rise they rise again with bud and
blossom rife,

To bask awhile in his warm smile, who is their lord
and life."

" All the cows bring forth are cattle—only now and
then is born

An authentic lord of pastures, with his shoulder-
scratching horn."

" When the soldier in the battle lays his life down for
    his king,
Unto Swarga's perfect glory such a deed his soul
    shall bring."

———

" 'Tis the fool who, meeting trouble, straightway Destiny
    reviles,
Knowing not his own misdoing brought his own mis-
    chance the whiles."

———

" ' Time-not-come ' and ' Quick-at-Peril,' these two fishes
    'scaped the net ;
' What-will-be-will-be,' he perished, by the fishermen
    beset."

———

" Sex, that tires of being true,
    Base and new is brave to you !
    Like the jungle-cows ye range,
    Changing food for sake of change."

———

" That which will not be will not be, and what is to be
    will be :
Why not drink this easy physic, antidote of misery ? "

" Whoso trusts, for service rendered, or fair words, an
    enemy,

  Wakes from folly like one falling in his slumber from
    a tree.'

———

"Fellow be with kindly foemen, rather than with
    friends unkind ;

  Friend and foeman are distinguished not by title but
    by mind."

———

" Whoso setting duty highest, speaks at need unwel-
    come things,

  Disregarding fear and favour, such an one may suc-
    cour kings."

———

" Brahmans for their lore have honour ; Kshattriyas for
    their bravery ;

  Vaisyas for their hard-earned treasure ; Sudras for
    humility."

———

" Seven foemen of all foemen, very hard to vanquish be :
  The Truth-teller, the Just-dweller, and the man from
    passion free,

Subtle, self-sustained, and counting frequent well-
 won victories,
And the man of many kinsmen—keep the peace with
 such as these."

" For the man with many kinsmen answers by them
 all attacks ;
As the bambu, in the bambus safely sheltered, scorns
 the axe."

———

" Whoso hath the gift of giving wisely, equitably, well;
 Whoso, learning all men's secrets, unto none his own
  will tell :
Whoso, ever cold and courtly, utters nothing that
 offends,
Such an one may rule his fellows unto Earth's
 extremest ends."

———

" Cheating them that truly ˈtrust you, 'tis a clumsy
 villany !
Any knave may slay the child who climbs and
 slumbers on his knee."

" Hunger hears not, cares not, spares not; no boon of
the starving beg;

When the snake is pinched with craving, verily she
eats her egg."

———

" Of the Tree of State the root
Kings are—feed what brings the fruit."

———

" Courtesy may cover malice; on their *heads* the wood-
men bring,

Meaning all the while to burn them, logs and faggots
—oh, my King!

And the strong and subtle river, rippling at the cedar's
foot,

While it seems to lave and kiss it, undermines the
hanging root."

———

" Weep not! Life the hired nurse is, holding us a
little space;

Death, the mother who doth take us back into our
proper place."

" Gone, with all their gauds and glories: gone, like

    peasants, are the Kings,

Whereunto this earth was witness, whereof all her

    record rings."

' For the body, daily wasting, is not seen to waste away,

    Until wasted; as in water set a jar of unbaked clay."

" And day after day man goeth near and nearer to his

    fate,

As step after step the victim thither where its slayers

    wait."

      " Like as a plank of drift-wood

        Tossed on the watery main,

      Another plank encountered,

        Meets,—touches,—parts again;

      So tossed, and drifting ever,

        On life's unresting sea,

      Men meet, and greet, and sever,

        Parting eternally."

" Halt, traveller! rest i' the shade: then up and leave
it!
Stay, Soul! take fill of love; nor losing, grieve it!"

" Each beloved object born
Sets within the heart a thorn,
Bleeding, when they be uptorn."

" If thine own house, this rotting frame, doth wither,
Thinking another's lasting—goest thou thither?"

" Meeting makes a parting sure,
Life is nothing but death's door."

" As the downward-running rivers never turn and never
stay,
So the days and nights stream deathward, bearing
human lives away."

" Bethinking him of darkness grim, and death's un-
shunnèd pain,
A man strong-souled relaxes hold, like leather soaked
in rain."

" From the day, the hour, the minute,
    Each life quickens in the womb;
Thence its march, no falter in it,
    Goes straight forward to the tomb."

" An 'twere not so, would sorrow cease with years ?
    Wisdom sees right what want of knowledge fears."

" Seek not the wild, sad heart! thy passions haunt it;
    Play hermit in thy house with heart undaunted;
    A governed heart, thinking no thought but good,
    Makes crowded houses holy solitude."

" Away with those that preach to us the washing off
        of sin—
    Thine own self is the stream for thee to make ablu-
        tions in :
    In self-restraint it rises pure—flows clear in tide of
        truth,
    By widening banks of wisdom, in waves of peace and
        truth."

Bathe there, thou son of Pandu! with reverence and
    rite,

For never yet was water wet could wash the spirit
    white."

———

" Thunder for nothing, like December's cloud,
Passes unmarked: strike hard, but speak not loud."

———

" Minds deceived by evil natures, from the good their
    faith withhold;

When hot conjee once has burned them, children blow
    upon the cold."

THE END.